I0828323

THE IDEA OF GOD AND SOCIAL IDEALS

BY THE SAME AUTHOR

THE SPIRITUAL PRINCIPLE OF THE ATONEMENT

THE FATHERHOOD OF GOD

CHRISTIAN RELIGION: ITS MEANING AND PROOF

GOD IN CHRIST JESUS: A STUDY OF ST. PAUL'S EPISTLE TO THE EPHESIANS

SONSHIP AND SALVATION

THE VICTORIAN TRANSFORMATION OF THEOLOGY

REMINISCENCES

&c.

THE IDEA OF GOD AND SOCIAL IDEALS

THE SOCIAL SERVICE LECTURE, 1938

BY

J. SCOTT LIDGETT,

C.H., M.A., D.D.

WIPF & STOCK · Eugene, Oregon

Wipf and Stock Publishers
199 W 8th Ave, Suite 3
Eugene, OR 97401

The Idea of God and Social Ideals
The Social Service Lecture, 1938
By Lidgett, J. Scott

ISBN 13: 978-1-5326-3510-6
Publication date 6/16/2017
Previously published by Epworth Press, 1938

CONTENTS

PREFACE

It was with reluctance that I undertook to give the Social Service Lecture of 1938, and to prepare this volume. Age and manifold duties made the acceptance of this task difficult, and have made its performance imperfect. I could not resist, however, the kind persuasion of my old and valued friend, Dr. W. F. Lofthouse, or the memory of the founder of this Lectureship, the late Mr. J. R. Beckly. Moreover, my mind was occupied with the subject of which I have endeavoured to treat just at the time when the invitation came, outlining in all the essentials what was already in my thought.

The volume is purely expository. Philosophic and psychological problems are suggested at many points of this exposition. They cannot be dealt with here, though I have discussed most of them, to the best of my ability, in my other theological books.

Such as it is, I send forth this book in the hope that it may be of service to those who are taking part in social endeavours at this critical period of human history, and as a confession, for what it may be worth, of the faith which has sustained me throughout a long career of public life and social service.

J. Scott Lidgett.

July 1938.

CHAPTER I

INTRODUCTORY

The object which the generous founder of the Beckly Trust had in view was to bring the convinced support of the Christian Church, and of Methodism in particular, to aid the cause of constructive social reform in all its manifold concerns. The first question, therefore, that arises is whether such concentration upon social reform is a true development and application of the Christian faith, or whether it involves a deflexion of the Church from its true aims and a lowering of its divinely-given spiritual ideals.

To the ordinary observer this question does not admit of an easy or confident answer. While he finds the Christian Church as a whole to be united in inculcating the moral standards of the New Testament in regard to the personal character and conduct of Christians, he is also confronted with serious divergences of thought and activity in regard to the wider social implications of these standards. These differences become more marked when such an observer examines the attitude of great bodies of Christians towards such systematic efforts to secure social reconstruction as seek to substitute constructive efforts to bring about social well-being for merely palliative remedies after evils have arisen. The latter have invariably evoked the sympathy and support of individual Christians, and have brought concerted enterprises into being whenever Christian faith has been enriched and inspired by the glow of Christian love. When, however, attempts have been made to arouse the State to comprehensive efforts for social reconstruction, and to co-operate with the State in effecting such reforms, Christian opinion has been divided, except when such moral interests are so obviously concerned as to compel the instant support of instinctive Christian piety.

Whenever anything more comprehensive has arisen, force of habit, in many, has withstood any adventure upon the unknown, fear of doubtful alliances has been awakened, and whole sections of well-intentioned people have shrunk from exchanging the limited advantages that they have experienced for the larger benefits which they have not experienced. The progressive urge comes into conflict with the caution which is apprehensive of the risks of change. Above all, many Christians, to whom Church associations have been the most vital and precious of all human relationships, have imagined that in passing beyond the frontiers of the Church they will be committed to such merely mundane considerations and methods as appear to them to be purely secular and unspiritual. Beyond such differences, and stimulated by them, conflicting philosophies have arisen. Eternity and time, spiritual values and material advantages, the faith which transcends the world and efforts which are immersed in the environing conditions of the world, are contrasted. Each of these alternatives has its philosophy. Each is contemptuous of the other. Each claims to represent the Christian faith. The philosophy of eternity, of spiritual values, and of transcendent faith claims the support of the New Testament, and treats the limitations of apostolic concern, essential and inevitable at the time, as of such permanent authority as to discountenance, or even inhibit, practical ideals and activities which had no scope in the ancient world.

The limitations imposed upon the early Christian Church by its secular conditions, the existing divisions of Christian opinion, and the judgement of the past by standards that have only become relevant in the present, have combined to provoke scornful condemnation of the Church, and even of the Christian faith, in the case of multitudes who have never studied the New Testament, are ignorant of history, and whose keen desire for social righteousness and betterment make them impatient and indignant in contemplating the imperfections and evils of our present State. Such people frequently charge the existing evils upon the Church, which is estimated by them as a Public Utility Society and found wanting. The Church, they say, has had nearly two thousand years in which to work, and behold the sorry result. Its influence has been an opiate; its doubtful and half-hearted benefits restricted to the elect; its effect, not to unite mankind, but to divide man into the hostile camps of the so-called sacred and the secular.

Far be it from us to deny that there is a measure of truth in this indictment. Incidentally, those who press it bear unwitting testimony to the potential influence of religion, to the character of Christ as the Founder and Object of the Christian faith, to the beneficent truths of His gospel, and to the position of the Christian Church as a powerful factor in human history. Yet, in their estimate, they overlook the forces of anti-Christ and its insidious corrosion of Christian life. They are also guilty of a flagrant inconsistency. While magnifying evolution as explanatory of Nature and man, they fail to apply the doctrine to the Christian Church as limiting its thought and activities by its relativity to the conditions and outlook of successive ages, and by the differing racial temperaments and stages of development among the peoples of the world. Christianity, like all else in human life, is still young. Its potentialities must be estimated by its principles and by their relevance to the present and future of mankind, as well as by its achievements when it has been *alive* and has had free scope.

The antinomy of Christian thought and life which has just been described has been recently dealt with by Dr. Reinhold Niebuhr of New York in a book entitled *An Interpretation of Christian Ethics*.[1] His book is deserving of careful study, for it is the fruit of extensive learning and deep reflection. Though the author's immediate object is the criticism of contrasted types of Christian outlook that are prevalent in the United States, it is of wider significance, since these types exist with certain modifications throughout the Christian world, and not least of all in this country.

Dr. Niebuhr's polemic is directed equally against what he terms Christian orthodoxy and Christian liberalism.

'Orthodox Christianity,' he says, 'with insights and perspectives in many ways superior to those of

[1] *An Interpretation of Christian Ethics*, by Reinhold Niebuhr (Student Christian Movement Press).

liberalism, cannot come to the aid of modern man, partly because its religious truths are still embedded in an outmoded science and partly because its morality is expressed in dogmatic and authoritarian moral codes' (p. 14).

On the other hand, 'The religion and ethics of the liberal Church are dominated by the desire to prove to its generation that it does not share the anachronistic ethics or believe the incredible myths of orthodox religion. Its energy for some decades has been devoted to the task of proving religion and science compatible, a purpose which it has sought to fulfil by disavowing the more incredible portion of its religious heritage and clothing the remainder in terms acceptable to the "modern mind" ' (p. 15). In contrast to both these types, Dr. Niebuhr contends that 'the distinctive contribution of religion to morality lies in its comprehension of the dimension of depth in life' (p. 15). Its effort is to bring the whole of reality and existence into some system of coherence. Hence there is tension between what is and what ought to be, a tension which must not be prematurely resolved. The attempt of liberal religion to do this results in its 'thinness' and superficiality. 'Failure to recognize the heights led modern Christianity to an equal blindness toward the darker depths of life' (p. 26). Higher religions are of two types, 'mystical' and 'mythical'. The former, in seeking to be rational, ends in such abstraction as to posit 'an ultimate reality beyond all rational forms'. Prophetic religion, just because it finds meaning and purpose in history, becomes mythical, and for the most part mistakes the truths embodied in the myths for events in history. The ethic of Jesus, which is 'the perfect fruit of prophetic religion', sets forth 'the ideal of love'. 'God is, therefore, love' (pp. 47–8). Our Lord's teaching is, in consequence, brought up against the inexorable fact of self-love, which is the 'natural will to survive', and this collision produces the sense of sin, which, while essentially bound up with man's finitude, is interpreted by religion as consisting in 'an evil will.' Yet, in consequence of the actual conditions of human life, the perfectionism of Jesus is practically impossible, and attempts to apply it in the realm of human life reduce its meaning and lead to the subtle substitution of lower and less meaningful principles, alike in politics, economics, and personal life. It remains, therefore, 'an impossible possibility', which has relevance to human life, but cannot be fulfilled in it. The Kingdom of God, as set forth by Jesus, 'is always a possibility in history, because its heights of pure love are organically related to the experience of love in all human life, but it is also an impossibility in history, and always beyond every historical achievement. Men living in nature and in the body will never be capable of the sublimation of egoism and the attainment of the sacrificial passion, the complete disinterestedness which the ethic of Jesus demands' (p. 42).

Perhaps the essential meaning of this book may be found in Dr. Inge's statement in his recently published *Anthology of the Christian Life* (*Freedom, Love, and Truth*): 'Christianity is a revolutionary idealism which estranges revolutionaries by its idealism, and conservatives by its drastic revaluation of earthly goods. Its function in social struggles is to take the sting out of such conflicts by setting its own standards before both sides.'

What is to be said of this apparently fundamental impasse, and of the antinomy between spirit and nature, with its outcome in contrasted types of religion, which are equally inadequate? To begin with, the hard-and-fast division of religious types into orthodoxy and liberalism, in emphasizing extremes, ignores the great intermediate realm in which both types, if not blended, qualify one another, not artificially, but in a living way. True catholicity of faith avoids both the rigidity and the fluidity, both the remoteness and the 'thinness', which are justly criticized. In the next place, Dr. Niebuhr's account of mystical religion is too purely intellectual to do justice either to its hidden springs or to its ultimate objective. His description may, on the whole, be true of neoplatonism, but only imperfectly represents typical Christian mysticism. It is more important to note that the book leaves the ethic of Jesus in a somewhat uncertain and, indeed, precarious position. Is Jesus the spiritually authoritative revealer and interpreter alike of the highest, inmost, and ultimate reality? Or is He the supreme idealist, the absoluteness of whose teaching is out of true proportion, being, indeed, incompatible with complete sanity, because out of keeping with the fundamental nature of the universe? If the latter, why does the idealism of Jesus so persistently press itself upon mankind and set up a permanent standard of what ought to be? Is not its relevancy the sign that it manifests a higher and real order of being, which, because it is the highest and most real, will eventually be fulfilled in human history, either under terrestrial conditions or in a succeeding order, which will be at once the fruit and the transformation of the present? All this is left, to the mind of the present writer, in uncertainty, though this may possibly be due to the fact that the book is limited to an interpretation of Christian ethics and does not attempt such a philosophy of the Christian religion as would integrate ethics in a consistent and satisfying whole.

The question, however, goes deeper. The author apparently cannot accept what he calls 'St. Paul's Christ-mysticism', because, according to him, it borders 'on the very edge of the magical' (p. 226). Yet without the consentient Christology of the Church, which is more than Pauline, the absoluteness of the ethic of Jesus remains doubtful, because it is insecurely based. Moreover, the New Testament is in accord with Dr. Niebuhr in treating the Christian ethic as 'an impossible possibility' apart from the new birth, 'the birth from above' of St. John, or the equivalent 'resurrection' of St. Paul. This possible transformation of human nature is left out of the picture by Dr. Niebuhr, yet no account of the ethic of Jesus can be complete without it. When this is admitted, and indeed insisted upon, the limitations of existent human nature may well be transcended, men may yet rise to the sacrificial heights which Dr. Niebuhr treats as impossible, and even the supposed rigidity of cosmic conditions may yield to the transforming influence of the Spirit, exerting its power as perfect love.

The contrast between what Dr. Niebuhr terms mystical and mythical religion has been recently treated by Dr. Joseph Needham as the opposition of Greek Neoplatonism and Hebrew apocalypticism in an article on 'The Common Ground between Christianity and Communism'.[1] In regard to this, Dr. Needham emphasizes the importance of 'the philosophical evaluation of time'. 'If time is illusory, unimportant, or evil, the trend of other-worldliness in Christianity becomes fundamental, earthly affairs lose their significance, and the Kingdom of Heaven is interpreted as a realm of mystical experience unconnected with concrete human relationships.' If, on the other hand, time be treated as significant, 'the Kingdom of God is no unearthly conceptual realm, but a just and happy social order', which draws towards it 'to work for its realization men of the most diverse types from all peoples of the world'. 'These two widely diverted trends', Dr. Needham says, 'have existed side by side in an uneasy union in the Christian religion since the first few centuries.' Here again we are presented with two unreconciled extremes to the neglect of intermediate positions in which they are more or less completely harmonized.

In face of these conflicting views, pressed upon us by two thoughtful and influential writers, it becomes necessary to examine the classic sources of the Christian religion in order, if possible, to discover an underlying unity, out of which both of these extremes have arisen, and by means of which the truth underlying each of them may be brought into organic spiritual coherence. It should be remarked at the outset that throughout the New Testament the mystical and the apocalyptic elements of the Christian religion are found side by side, and that the apostolic writers had no sense that they stood

[1] *Spectator*, October 30, 1936.

in 'an uneasy union' with one another. For example, St. Paul, in writing to the Church at Philippi, and with the relationship of imperial Rome with its colonies in his mind, declares in the same sentence that 'the State of which we are citizens (πολίτευμα) is in heaven, from whence also we look for the Saviour, the Lord Jesus Christ' (Philippians iii. 20). Here the mystical and the apocalyptic are treated as the inseparable parts of one spiritual whole, and this is characteristic of the general tenor of his teaching. Moreover, the Apostle's practical injunctions are so closely bound up with both these aspects of the Christian religion as to form a vital bond between them, and to dismiss any conception of an 'Interims-Ethik' as entirely foreign to his belief. In consonance with the prophetic teaching of the Old Testament, Christian ethics rest upon the character of God, and are, therefore, unaffected save in their applications by secular changes. While their application is relative to the order of the world, in principle they are absolute and eternal, because they spring out of relationships not primarily to the creatures, but to the Creator.

On closer examination it will be found that there is a third element of which due account must be taken, namely the inward. 'The Kingdom of God', St. Paul declares, 'is not eating and drinking, but righteousness and peace and joy in the Holy Spirit' (Romans xiv. 17). Thus the inward, the mystical, and the prospective are treated as three essential and mutually consistent parts of Christian faith and life. A more intimate study of the New Testament will reveal the nature of the bond that unites them.

1. In the first place must be set the inwardness of

the Christian religion. Our Lord is reported to have said, 'The Kingdom of God cometh not with observation: neither shall they say, Lo, here! or there! for lo, the Kingdom of God is within you' (Luke xvii. 20, 21). It is, of course, possible to translate the Greek preposition as meaning 'among' you, but this is seriously to weaken the force of the contrast that is so obviously intended. As Dr. Niebuhr remarks, the ethic of Jesus 'has only a vertical dimension between the loving will of God and the will of man' (p. 49). The Kingdom of God means His effective rule in the hearts of men, and, therefore, throughout their life and conduct. It involves such spiritual union between God and man as makes, and can alone make, the sovereign authority of God the immanent spring of a response which makes 'All's Law' to be 'All's Life', because 'the love of God has been shed abroad in our hearts'. Yet throughout the teaching both of our Lord and of His apostles this union between God and men in love is not left in this formlessness. It is everywhere set forth as the union and fellowship of the Father and His sons. Our Lord's life, teaching, and spirit are throughout governed by this conscious relationship between God as His Father and Himself as the Son. This conscious experience is His specific gift to His followers. It is by the experience of this Fatherly-filial relationship that the inwardness of the Kingdom of God must be explained. It is the inmost secret, the vital meaning, of the Christian religion. Theology, religion, ethics are all transformed, throughout the New Testament, by the illumination and inspiration of this supreme and all-embracing relationship. The human relationship of fatherhood and sonship is everywhere treated as so constituted in God that it is the most adequate representation of a mystical relationship in which the most intimate fellowship is enjoyed on the basis of personal distinction, divine creatorship, and such human subordination as contains within itself the sense of kinship and affinity with God.

2. This divine sonship gives to the inwardness of the Kingdom of God two essential characteristics. It is both transcendent and forthgoing. Its 'treasure' is in heaven, but its immediate objective is on earth. It brings together the supreme values of the eternal order and the importance of the historic process in time. This twofold reference is the essential meaning of sonship. It seeks at once to pursue and to enjoy the highest, and to manifest it by uplifting and transforming the terrestrial order. Only in this combination is the integrity and wholeness of spiritual life to be realized and displayed. Heaven is the sphere of absolute values that are realized and active in the living God, and are participated in by those who are in fellowship with Him as His sons. Yet these values are implanted in true human life, are organic with it, and can only be pursued in so far as they gain practical expression in character and social conduct.

The typical example of this fundamental combination is to be found in our Lord, who 'went about preaching the gospel of the Kingdom' and 'doing good'. Hence His consciousness was at once mystic and apocalyptic, because it was perfectly filial. The relationship of eternity to time remains a philosophic problem. Yet each is real, and God who 'inhabiteth eternity' comes forth as Creator to fulfil an eternal purpose in time and history. He is both transcendent and immanent because He is Love. So, also, it is with His Son. Hence the life of His followers is also essentially twofold. The author of the Epistle to the Hebrews says, almost in the same breath, 'Ye are come unto Mount Zion, the city of the living God, the heavenly Jerusalem', and 'To do good and to communicate [that is, to share] forget not, for with such sacrifices God is well pleased'. This practical temper and conduct alone correspond with the 'vertical' relationship that exists for men with 'the Father, from whom every family constituted by fatherhood' (πατριά) 'is named'; that is, derives its nature.

3. Yet it is the characteristic faith of the Christian religion that, in thus combining the mystic and the apocalyptic, the followers of Christ are neither supreme nor alone in playing their part in human history. Christ is for them the supreme actor in human history. The world will finally be judged by the spiritual values of His perfect life. The age-long conflict of human history is between Christ and anti-Christ, between self-giving and self-loving. Human life, and even the cosmic order, will eventually be transformed by the Spirit of Christ, and the discord between them will be finally harmonized, after the conflict has played its part in evoking and perfecting the eternal values of divine Love. This final consummation will be the triumph, not of men, but of Christ.

This final triumph can for the present be only scenically depicted, if at all, with the inherent imperfections and externality by which such picturing must needs be marked. Yet even this picturing, though misleading when treated with fundamentalist literalism, enshrines great spiritual truths. Its 'treasure' is held 'in earthen vessels', for 'we know not yet what we shall be'. Owing to their limitations, men have presented as irrational alternatives what are to be held together in a spiritual whole. This whole, when truly apprehended, accepts 'the one far-off divine event to which the whole creation moves', as the goal both of religious and of ethical conduct, and does so just because of the filial spirit, which 'seeks the things that are above, where Christ is seated at the right hand of God'.

This point of view is incidentally illustrated and at the same time enforced by our Lord's declaration, 'Verily I say unto you, whosoever shall not receive the Kingdom of God as a little child, he shall not enter therein' (Mark x. 15; Matthew xix. 13; Luke xviii. 17). Two features stand out clearly in this saying. In the first place, it is the receptivity of a little child that is insisted upon. Its innocence, simplicity, and, above all, trustfulness make it receptive of kindness, instruction, and influence. The frankness with which it receives is linked with the spontaneity by which it gives expression to what it has received and acts upon it.

In the second place, the little child responds to an actual and encompassing environment, whether of persons or of things, which invites and rewards its trust. Childlikeness is not an abstract quality, but an attitude of receptive fellowship with the child's surroundings. So it is, our Lord points out, with the Kingdom of God. It is the real and encompassing environment of men, offering itself to their apprehension, trust, and obedience. It is the

Kingdom of 'our Father', and, therefore, appeals to men with authoritative love and even congeniality. It must, consequently, be 'received' with the same directness and simplicity with which a little child receives the love, the teaching, and the guidance of its parents. And, in accordance with the attitude of true childlikeness, this receptivity is both continuous and practical. What is given and received becomes the substance of what is believed, the inspiration of what is done. Childlikeness of spirit enables men to experience the presence and grace of God; His guidance and enablement; above all, His love, with all the values it discloses. It then prompts them so to act upon this experience that the Kingdom of God, thus received, is made manifest in lives that give living expression to it through all the activities of their social environment.

It is important and easy to pass from this survey to consider the constitution and spiritual significance of the Christian Church, as its life is described and prescribed in the New Testament.

1. In the first place, its life is communal. The Church is neither sacerdotal, prelatical, nor individualist. It is a 'fellowship', based upon the apostolic doctrine, and finding both its support and its expression in 'the breaking of bread, and the prayers' (Acts ii. 42). Its fellowship springs from the common relationship of its members to God as Father and Saviour. While, therefore, the fellowship is profoundly spiritual, it is frankly and naturally human. It may distinguish between the spiritual and the physical, but it never divides them. It does not promote the higher by neglect of the lower. On the contrary, it elevates the concerns of bodily

life into the realm of the spiritual, since even the body is 'the temple of the Holy Ghost' (1 Corinthians vi. 19). Hence the very height and intensity of the spiritual fellowship of the Church make it solicitous for the physical well-being and the material security of its members. Moreover, this comprehensive concern for men, as men, includes the development of their reason. The *Truth* is the object of their faith, and, therefore, its intelligent apprehension 'in all wisdom and spiritual understanding' (Colossians i. 9) is a vital element in the Communion of the Saints. Great emphasis is laid upon knowledge throughout the New Testament, and, while this knowledge is that of inmost experience and not that of mere information, yet it must, of necessity, include the intellect, and, therefore, the rational coherence that alone can integrate human life in its divine, human, and cosmic relationships. For the sake of such integration, the Fellowship of the Church must seek to apprehend the wholeness of the universe in and for God.

2. The Fellowship of the Church, while highly distinctive, is never exclusive. The Eucharist, as the central rite of the Church, displays and promotes the essential meaning of the Fellowship. Its simple action contains an epitome of Christian truth and life. But the preaching – the proclamation of the gospel – not merely for the edification of the Church, but as conveying the divine invitation and summons to the whole world, is an essential element of Church life. This proclamation involves and should set forth the truth that all men everywhere are destined by 'the goodness and philanthropy of God our Saviour' (Titus iii. 4) to participate in the

fellowship which is enjoyed by the children of God and is displayed in the Eucharist. This catholicity is an essential mark of the Church of Christ, and this catholicity should never shed its comprehension of human nature as a whole, consisting in the union of body, soul, and spirit, and the service of a love which gives by sharing, and by sharing is not impoverished but enriched.

It follows from all this that social service is an outstanding consequence and expression of Christian faith and life. It is deeply grounded in, and should be fashioned by, the following fundamental facts:

(1) That mankind is one body, one family, and destined to become one commonwealth. Its unity is already realized in the Church as a Catholic Fellowship in Christ. The Church is the earnest and the agent of the eternal purpose of God 'to sum up all things in Christ' (Ephesians i. 10).

(2) That this one body, this family, which is potentially universal, springs forth from 'the Father, from whom every family constituted by fatherhood is named' (Ephesians iii. 15).

(3) That this one body, this family, is not outside the life of God, but is grounded in His Eternal, Incarnate, and Sacrificial Son, our Lord Jesus Christ.

(4) Hence, that self-offering in communal service is the sacrifice acceptable to God. 'To do good and to share forget not, for with such sacrifices God is well pleased' (Hebrews xiii. 16). 'Let us do good unto all men, and especially unto them who are of the household of faith' (Galatians vi. 20), the preference being given to the latter because the intimacy of the relationship involves prior responsibility, greater

accessibility, and truer sharing. For sacrifices to be acceptable to God they must be acts of filial fellowship, and this can only be the case in so far as they fulfil and set forth the vital relationship that exists between God, the offerer, and those to whom the service is rendered – this relationship consisting in Fatherhood, sonship, and brotherhood.

The life of Christ's Church is collectively priestly and prophetic. There is neither contrast nor separation between the two, for they are the spiritual expression of the Fatherly-filial relationship, the significance of which has already been explained. The self-giving of the Church, both personal and collective, is, in the first place, its sacrifice of self-surrender to God, in accord with His character, mind, and will. It is, therefore, priestly and sacrificial. This self-giving, however, must needs be in fellowship with the purpose of God, 'who willeth that all men shall be saved and come to the knowledge of the truth' (1 Timothy ii. 4). Hence the filial sacrifice to God, as priestly, is seen in the prophetic ministry of the Church in forwarding the divine purpose, with which it is at one. And this prophetic ministry is fulfilled not in word only, but in such influence and activities as cause 'the goodness and philanthropy of God' continuously and effectively to appear. As in the case of our Lord, the word of the Church must 'become flesh and tabernacle' among men, for their enlightenment, redemption, and well-being.

What, then, should be the attitude of the Christian Church to secular progress, as so conceived? The conception of progress is not Christian in its origin, nor has it been Christian in its development. It was first launched by Lucretius in a magnificent passage in which he interpreted human history as the record of men slowly advancing – '*pedetentim progredientes*' (Lucretius, v. 1448 *et seq.*) – in a definite and desirable direction, and infers that the process will continue indefinitely. The development of the doctrine has been humanist and not theological. Its content postulates a natural and normal process of development, by which mankind will ultimately attain complete realization – individual and collective, moral and intellectual – such attainment implying also complete adjustment between men and their terrestrial environment.

Obviously the doctrine has to encounter great difficulties. History does not reveal any such sustained and self-enclosed human advance. Civilizations have waxed, waned, and perished. Catastrophic set-backs have taken place. Periods of apparent stagnation and even of the absence or exhaustion of an impulse to seek progress have not seldom occurred. At the best, progress has only been partial, both in time and space. There have been gaps and breakdowns, with only an imperfect resumption of suspended endeavours and a partial carry-over of previous gains. Hence the history of civilization offers some support to the dictum of Freeman that 'in history, every step in advance has also been a step backward'. If evolution be accepted as a natural process, it appears to be limited both in dynamic and in range, while it is shadowed by counterbalancing phenomena, which are attributable to the same general laws and due to an equally natural process. Furthermore, the presence of what appears to be chance and contingency in human affairs cannot be ignored, as Voltaire long ago pointed out. Finally, the assumption that the environment to which life must be adjusted is a fixed and unchanging datum, and that, therefore, the task of progress is definite in its nature and limited in its demands, is clearly erroneous. The environment of men is constantly changing, partly in consequence of what are termed natural causes, and partly as the result of human efforts to transform it. Hence no law of progress has been discovered, and it may, perhaps, be concluded that the idea of progress is an assumption due to the inborn confidence of men of exceptional energy, of sanguine disposition, and of practical beneficence thinking and working in comparatively peaceful times.

Hence the Christian religion has never accepted the idea of progress as it has been expounded by secularist thinkers. And this for two conclusive reasons. First of all, because it cannot contemplate human and cosmic life as a self-enclosed system, independent of the creative sovereignty and the spiritual influence of God. And, in the second place, because Christian religion cannot ignore the fact of sin, and the consequent conflict of Christ and anti-Christ, of regenerate and unregenerate human nature, of self-giving and self-love.

Yet a truer and more stable foundation for what is essential in the idea of progress is furnished by the Christian religion itself.

1. It rests upon, and springs from, faith in the eternal purpose of God and upon 'the goodness and philanthropy of God our Saviour which have appeared' in our Lord Jesus Christ. This purpose has been revealed, not in abstract thought, but in the character, work, and influence of a supreme

personality, who is vitally and permanently active in the history of mankind. The beneficence of the divine purpose has been so effectively revealed in the experience of believers that they have become 'workers together with God' in realizing His beneficent purpose for man. This eternal purpose supplies St. Paul with a distinctive doctrine of creative evolution. It was 'in the dispensation of the fulness of the times' that our Lord appeared as the fulfilment of a great preparatory process and the inaugurator of a new era of divine manifestation and human salvation (Ephesians i. 10).

2. There is, therefore, for Christians a ceaseless urge towards progress. It springs, however, not from the inherent qualities of human nature, secularly conceived, but from that nature as regenerated, reinforced, and guided by the immanent Spirit of Christ. The influence of His Spirit enables His followers to seize opportunities, to overcome obstacles, and to utilize all available instruments to give effect to the dictates of the love of God 'shed abroad' in their hearts and actuating them to sacrificial effort for the redemption and fulfilment of human nature, in the light of the eternal values and of their temporal demands.

3. Finally, the fact of the Incarnation, and the history of the Incarnate Son of God, set the ideal standard of Christian aims and methods for the betterment of mankind. Hope has been lifted by the gospel from the despised and distrusted position it held in Greek estimation into association with faith and love as one of the primary and indispensable graces of the Christian life. It is at once a divinely imparted gift, an invincible armament, and an

imperative duty of Christians. Hope is the fulfilment of faith, and gives objectivity to the aims and efforts of love. Hope is interfused by its sister graces, informed and balanced by them. Its object and ground is God (1 Peter i. 21). It confidently anticipates the triumph in the Kingdom of our Father of the supreme spiritual values that are revealed to faith and embraced by love. Its satisfaction, therefore, is heavenly, not earthly. Yet the temper of hope and the attitude of hopefulness are evoked by faith in the divine order and purpose, the meaning of which has been revealed in the Incarnation of the Son of God and in the essential truths that are enshrined in it. The Incarnation displays the vital connexion not only between God and man, but between the spiritual and the natural, the eternal and the secular order. Christians are bidden to 'rejoice in hope of the glory of God' (Romans v. 2). Yet the glory of God is not altogether reserved, either by prophets or apostles, for a final order sharply distinguished from the present. It is progressive and pervasive because it is spiritual. The manifestation of the glory of God was the motive that moved Him to creatorship, and to creatorship by means of self-bestowal upon His universe in all its parts and all its stages. The very fact, therefore, that Christian hope is fixed upon the eternal makes it a persistent and all-embracing attitude towards the experience and process of time in all its parts. Hope then becomes a divine incentive to progress, and yet hope that is fixed upon God maintains the supremacy of spiritual values, is armed with invincible patience, and grows in wisdom and knowledge. The very fact that faith is fixed on the eternal constrains those who cherish it to make the existing order progressively an adequate environment, expression, and instrument of the spiritual – that is, the eternal life.

The fact that the religion of Christ is far removed alike from Epicurean hedonism and from Stoic indifference, that it has discovered and experienced rich spiritual values in suffering, does not for a moment mean that the suffering of the world, so far as it is preventable, is to pass unchallenged. Rather is it the case that part of the beneficial discipline of suffering is that it incites mankind to search out and apply such remedies for suffering as God is placing, and will place, within human reach.

It is by no means intended to suggest that religion, even the religion of Christ, is identical with ethics and the social reforms to which ethics can by itself be instrumental. Ethics in isolation is as departmental as science, and as incomplete. It is conditioned by the actual organization of human society, as such, with its activities, affections, and needs. Yet the very fact that the religion of Christ conveys that sense of kinship between God and man of which Fatherhood, sonship, and brotherhood are the watchwords, brings to morality loftier and more constraining motives, greater wealth of content, as well as a marvellous combination of rigidity and elasticity which is beyond the reach of the ordinary moralist.

With this introductory statement the way is clear to consider the relation of the Idea of God to Social Ideals as it is set forth in Holy Scripture, as it has been illustrated in Christian history, and as it has entered into the complex life of recent times.

CHAPTER II

EXPOSITORY

In considering the influence of the Idea of God upon Social Ideals, certain facts may, at the outset, be taken for granted as generally agreed. These fundamental agreements may be stated as follows:

1. That the ordering of human society has, until recent times, been based upon, fashioned, and cemented by accepted and authoritative religious beliefs, and that this is still the case with some peoples of mankind, even though these beliefs are more widely challenged than hitherto.

2. That a conscious and concerted effort to bring about the betterment of human society has arisen and become dominant in recent times, especially in democratic communities. This concerted effort has been stimulated by the growing sense of human needs and possibilities, and has been both fostered and made universal in its scope by the deepening of humane sympathy. The belief that such betterment is possible has been developed and made comprehensive by the growth of knowledge, scientific in theory and made applicable to the needs of men through the arts of life.

3. That this movement has given rise to ideals of what human society should become, whether visionary or scientific, whether reforming or revolutionary.

4. That the urge both to the acceptance of these ideals and to the duty of carrying them into practical

effect has been, at the outset, prophetic, inspired by spiritual beliefs and ethical motives, which have been to a large extent derived from Christian sources.

5. And, finally, that the continuance of this urge, when it has ceased to be avowedly religious, and even when it has been conceived as a reaction against accepted religions, beliefs, and practice, has been due to the continued influence of certain assumptions that have been inherited from a religious tradition, which is still operative, even though its formulation may have become apparently secular.

The hope that prompts to these social efforts, the faith that the universe will make a beneficent response to them, the sense that these efforts *ought* at all costs to be made, are evidence that the 'Age of Reason' depends, after all, upon faith, with its venture upon the unknown, and especially upon what is, in reality, the beneficent purposiveness of the universe as a whole, of which mankind is not the victim or the slave, but the heir and the interpretative reason. Moreover, it is impossible in this reference to overlook the potency of love, which has come to be something far more and far higher than mere natural affection, and is now, however often its dictates may be violated by human self-will, the supreme and organizing arbiter of the meaning of righteousness, and the indispensable condition of eventual social well-being. Thus faith, hope, and love supply the essential presuppositions which, proclaimed by prophets, are subsequently articulated by reason, arouse the enthusiasm of multitudes, and direct the practical policies of men.

How are all these facts to be explained? Only by

the patient study of history and by reflection upon the evidence that history supplies.

To begin with, it must be affirmed that social ideals, in so far as they are treated as ends in themselves, involve the recognition of the supreme value of human personalities, the worth of human society, and the vital connexion of these two. This threefold unity has won its way to the foreground of human apprehension through the influence of religion, with its testimony to the nature of the universe as constituted in and by God. Religion has been, according to its own characteristic confession, the human response to divine revelation. The sense of the supreme value of human personalities and of the worth of human society as bound up with the perfecting of these personalities in the fellowship inspired by love and fashioned by righteousness has arisen through the revelation of God as sovereign Personality, as holy and adorable Perfection, and of God as standing in such spiritual relations with men as at once to uphold, order, and inspire individual persons, and to preside over the society in and for which human personalities are to be preserved, exercised, and perfected. This means that the creative source of the social ideals, at first proclaimed by individuals, then promoted by voluntary societies, and finally adopted as the objectives of political action, must be sought in the Christian religion as inheriting the revelation of the Old Testament and consummating it. From no other religious source have lofty and far-reaching social ideals arisen, or could they have arisen, so as to inspire and guide the forward movement of mankind. Christianity is the outcome of Hebrew and

Jewish presuppositions, and without them the sense that the service of God and the service of man are indissolubly connected would never have come into being. The significance of human personality and its social consequences were realized in and through the Idea of God as Supreme Personality, as adorable because of His spiritual and ethical perfection, and as so creatively sovereign that He is at once the fatherly source and end, the law and the life of His creatures. Every stage of Old Testament revelation contributed to this result, as may be briefly shown.

It is necessary, therefore, to take note of the successive stages of Old Testament religion and its consummation in the New Testament in order that we may see how the Idea of God became of such moment to social ideals as to furnish the faith that has consciously inspired them in the past, and that is still active, even if unacknowledged, in the assumptions that continue to support and guide the social ideals of the present.

I. THE IDEA OF GOD AS DEVELOPED IN THE OLD TESTAMENT

1. It is the fashion to depreciate early Hebrew religion as mere tribalism, because God was set forth as 'the God of Abraham, the God of Isaac, and the God of Jacob, the God of our fathers'. That this conception was primitive and imperfect goes without saying. Yet the emphasis it laid upon the personality both of God and of the patriarchs, upon His comradely leadership over them and their concerns, and upon the living bond that united Him and them

under His directive and fostering Providence, laid the indispensable foundation of religious faith, not as cosmic explanation – the result of a primitive philosophy – but as living experience of a personal relationship, in which the Self-giving of God made Him not only supreme over, but 'deeply interfused' with, individual men and with their society, if only tribal. Their life as a tribal family was grounded in God, and the fathers stood in personal fellowship with Him. The inwardness and homeliness of this faith made it the indispensable foundation of all that followed in advancing revelation and spiritual consciousness. Only the deep inwardness of their initial faith enabled men to apprehend the Sovereignty of God in its all-comprehending nature as their knowledge of the universe became extended. Their social life became more complex, both in national and international relations, as their powers of reason and reflection were developed. Yet the primitive faith continued to underlie and fashion their attitude to life and to the world. It had the power both to deepen and to expand with the enlargement of their horizons and the growth of their responsibilities.

2. The next movement of the development is to be found in Mosaism, the Religion of the Covenant. This stage again emphasized the Personality of God, for it was in the exercise of His sovereign freedom that he chose Israel for a unique relationship to Himself. That relationship was morally conditioned by the Ten Commandments, which, in uniting the exclusive service of God with the duties of man, gave an indirect but striking suggestion of the character of God. The Personality of God in the exercise of

His sovereign freedom thus displayed in the Covenant was extended to the doctrine of His Creatorship. 'In the beginning God *created* the heavens and the earth.' The universe is not the emanation of His being, but the effect of His purposive will. Supreme and free Personality is, therefore, the master fact of the universe, and is truly, though imperfectly, reflected by the development of personality in men.

3. It remained for the revelation and religion of the Old Testament to characterize the Personality of God, whose supremacy over His people sprang out of His creative sovereignty of the universe. This was accomplished by the great prophetic succession, of which Deuteronomy, Amos, Hosea, and Isaiah are the outstanding and living monuments. In particular, the righteousness of God was proclaimed by Amos, His mercy, tenderness, and patience by Hosea, and these were so combined in the great prophecies of Isaiah as to furnish the material for the sublime Theism of Isaiah xl, in which the Old Testament doctrine of God – of His character, His creatorship, and His relationships to the universe and mankind – was summed up in the magnificent display of His glory as consisting in the free and unfailing Self-giving of His grace.

It is well to consider the development of the Old Testament Idea of God more fully, even at the risk of some repetition, for everything depends upon it. The Old Testament prophets brought into complete unity two contrasted elements in the doctrine of Theism. Ultimately, what may be called, with due reverence, the Transcendent Humanity of God occupies the foreground of religious faith and experience. God in His eternal perfection is worshipful;

above all, because in His essential Nature He *is* what men are destined *to become*. His relationship to His people consists in His disclosing to them progressively the glory of His perfection, and enjoining upon them the supreme task and duty of becoming comformable to it in character and conduct. His grace is shown, not only in His mercy and forgiveness, but in the Self-giving that goes forth to them, revealing His glory and imparting it to them. Yet 'Holy is He'. There are unapproachable heights and inexhaustible riches in His perfection that must for ever surpass human apprehension, however divinely illuminated and empowered. For men at their highest and best there must remain a beyond in the character of God, which clothes His majesty with mystery, and makes Him the source and spring of an illimitable wonder of Self-giving in revelation and in human salvation through fulfilment. Yet what is believed and known of God is true and trustworthy. The mystery that cannot be disclosed to finite creatures is the well-spring of what is knowable by men. The highest that is revealed in spiritual experience is a true manifestation of the perfection from which it springs. His being and character are not to be sought by the way of negation, but by ever-growing affirmations of which human comprehension is a faithful, though imperfect, reflection. Hence for the prophets and saints of the Old Testament, the sense that God must always stand *above* them does not mean that He stands *over against* them. God is 'Other' than they; yet not 'Altogether Other'. Awe and shrinking are overborne and dismissed by the ethical content of the Revelation, and by the fellowship with His people into which God enters, even as the Law-giver, who commands, 'Be ye holy, as I am holy', and, still more, by the grace which brings knowledge of Him and likeness to Him within their reach.

1. First of all, then, comes the Revelation of the Transcendent and Supreme Personality of God. The Revelation of the Name of Jahweh, '*I am that I am*', leaves Him uncharacterized save as supreme, self-consistent, unchangeable Personality. Creation is dependent upon Him, not He upon it.

2. The very conception of the Covenant, as an agreement into which God enters with His people, in like manner emphasizes personality in them as well as in Him. Israel as a people becomes a social unit bound together by the common will of consentient personalities.

3. On this basis of consentient personalities, the character of God becomes His law, and His law becomes His people's life. His attributes become their standards. His relationships to mankind and to the world become, in a subordinate but accordant sense, theirs. It is as righteous, true, and merciful that He is revealed as the Living God. There is such kinship between God and His people that they are called to be His 'witnesses'. Because of the universal beneficence of God it comes about that He can say to Abraham, 'In thee shall all families of the earth be blessed' (Genesis xii. 3).

4. The intrinsic worth of human personality, springing as it does from the divine, is further emphasized by the obligations to care for the poor, the widows, and the fatherless, again and again insisted upon by the prophets. This care is treated both as an individual duty and a civic responsibility.

It is the human expression of the compassionate concern of Jahweh. The value of religion is measured by the fulfilment of this social responsibility.

5. Thus, for the prophets, religion consisted, above all, in the ethical expression and the social application of the perfection of God in beneficence and loving kindness to men. Both the community and individual men were held morally responsible for this conduct. They were subject to divine approval, or judgement according as they fulfilled or disregarded it. Moral responsibility for the conditions of social well-being is one of the key rules of Old Testament prophecy.

It is nowadays the fashion to say that the ancient world did not possess the conception of personality, and hardly its sense. This statement is only true if the Old Testament be left out of account. Whatever may have been the origin and the original meaning of the name of God, Jahweh in familiar use, the Book of Exodus makes plain the significance which attached to it. 'I am that I am' is its standard definition for the faith of Israel. 'Thus shalt thou say unto the children of Israel, *I am* hath sent *me* unto *you*' (Exodus iii. 14). This saying emphasizes personality at every point; personality in God as the subject of moral perfection and the source of sovereign will; personality in His prophetic messenger, and personality in His people as being the subjects alike of spiritual and moral obligation and of divine redemption. The sense of individual responsibility, sin, and guilt which finds such poignant expression in many of the Psalms is conclusive evidence of all this.

When Old Testament religion at its highest proclaimed the divine demand, 'Be ye holy, for I am holy', it presented the full prophetic connotation of the fatherly sovereignty of God – His righteousness, mercy, and love towards men – as the moral and social standard for men and the lasting meaning of true religion. It was as the consummation and conservation of all this that our Lord, speaking out of His unique consciousness of divine Sonship, gave to mankind the Lord's Prayer, addressed to 'our Father, which art in heaven', and reaching its climax in the petition, 'Thy kingdom come. Thy will be done, as in heaven, so in earth'. It was in the light of all this that St. Paul spoke of our Lord as 'the Image of God'.

It was because of this revelation and fulfilment that the Idea of God furnished to Christianity its ideals of social service, its standards and its aims. They could be drawn from no other religious source, sustained by no other faith, and inspired by no lower or lesser meaning. Polytheism, however brilliant it became in the literature rather than the religion of ancient Greece, could give no such guidance and inspiration to social development, because its gods were overshadowed by impersonal destiny, because, at the best, they were imperfectly ethicized, because of the limitations of their respective spheres, and because of their conflicting characteristics. Even the growing ascendancy of Zeus was, in this respect, unavailing; for he never completely transcended the naturalism of his origin, which stood in the way of his ever becoming a supremely spiritual and ethical ideal.

Similarly, Indian religious philosophy, however

mystical, and neoplatonism, however profound, could supply no such social inspiration, because the impersonality of supreme Deity was incompatible with any adequate realization of the reality, meaning, and worth either of human personalities or, therefore, of the possibilities of their society. The compassionateness of the Buddha could only prompt to kindliness, and not to progress, for his pessimism and agnosticism directed him to the surrender of personality, and to the transitoriness of human society. The ethical loftiness of Zarathustra so emphasized dualism and conflict as both cosmic and human as to negate any possibility of the eventual triumph of the good, conceived as perfect love in the history of mankind. Finally, the emphasis laid by Mohammed upon will, might, and fate has prevented Mohammedism – despite its Hebrew and Christian inheritance – from adopting progressive ideals. The acceptance of these ideals by hitherto Mohammedan States has, therefore, involved a total breach with the Moslem religion.

All these defects have stood in the way of social progress, instead of furthering it, since the lack of ethical content in theology and religion must always hinder the due recognition alike of the claims of human personality, wherever and however imperfectly it exists, and of the nature of human society, as the ever-growing fellowship of free personalities. Only the faith of the sovereign Personality of God and of His free Self-giving as the source and the significance of human personality can avail to give the ideals of social service. It is just the emphasis so laid by Hebrew religion, as fulfilled in the Christian faith, that has made the ideal of a truly Christian civilization the foundation upon which religion and citizenship can go hand in hand, and upon which they can securely rest. Christian ethics, if their principles be fully embraced and their essential presuppositions be accepted, are the only means of social safety, stability, and progress. They are so deeply founded in reason and reality that, instead of ossifying past traditions, they call men to the adventurous reflection that will guide and stimulate courageous endeavours to transform an imperfect and unsatisfactory civilization in their light.

II. GOD AS KING

The history of Israel was dominated from first to last, and despite all perversions, by the faith of the Lordship of Jahweh, and of His ever-active control over His people, commanding and counselling, judging and saving them. The sense of nationhood had first dawned upon the Hebrew tribes in Egypt and in the wilderness under the prophetic leadership of Moses, who spoke, acted, and judged the people in the name and through the ceaseless revelation of Jahweh. When the loosely compacted tribes occupied their scattered settlements in the Holy Land, their sense of unity was fitfully aroused and slowly developed by prophets, judges, and military leaders, who exercised their authority in the name of Jahweh, and won the allegiance of the people through kindling their faith in Him. God was, therefore, the supreme and living source of authority and of law. His law was communicated to them by

His messengers in living teaching for practical applications to public and private situations and concerns as they arose. He was their refuge and strength in emergencies, their sovereign counsellor in national affairs. The conception of kingship was familiar to them because of its actual existence elsewhere. This conception embodied, in general, supreme authority, protective and aggressive leadership, competent direction, and a certain though variable fatherliness, which made the king, in the Homeric phrase, the 'shepherd' of his people, the custodian of their order and well-being. It was, therefore, with this conception in mind that Samuel said, when the people, impressed by the sense of the practical efficiency of monarchy elsewhere, demanded a king, 'When ye saw that Nahash the king of the children of Ammon came against you, ye said unto me, Nay, but a king shall reign over us; when Jahweh your God was your king'. In acceding to the popular demand, the prophet went on to say, 'And behold, Jahweh hath set a king over you', and added an exhortation in which the over-kingship of Jahweh was emphatically asserted. The people were to 'fear Jahweh, and serve Him, and hearken unto His voice' (1 Samuel xii. 12 *et seq.*). Hence the Kingship of Jahweh was reaffirmed, and the importance of the prophetic office asserted, as the means by which the sovereign commandments of Jahweh were to be continuously upheld through the spiritual and moral guidance and injunctions to be conveyed alike to king and people by His inspired messengers. Thus, throughout the subsequent history, the prophets held a spiritual ascendancy over the nation, and emphasized the truth that Israel was the people of Jahweh, that their supreme obligation was to their heavenly, and not to their earthly, king.

A twofold effect upon subsequent Old Testament prophecy resulted from this momentous constitutional change. On the one hand, the direct sovereignty of Jahweh was emphasized by certain of the prophets. For example, the assurance was given that 'there Jahweh will be with us in majesty, a place of broad rivers and streams; wherein shall go no galley with oars, neither shall gallant ship pass thereby. For Jahweh is our judge, Jahweh is our lawgiver, Jahweh is our King; He will save us' (Isaiah xxxiii. 21–3). On the other hand, both the achievements and the failures of the earthly monarch opened the way to the revelation of the coming advent of the Messianic King, who should fulfil the ideal of kingship in character, communion with God, and saviourship of His people. Under His rule, and by the influence of His Spirit, the ideal city and nation should appear, in perfect fellowship with God and in complete conformity to His will. They were thus to become the adequate earthly witness to His character, and enjoy the blessedness that can only result from full atonement with a finally manifested God. The Kingship of God, therefore, contained, in view of His character and His relationship to the world, both a pattern of life, to be immediately exemplified, and also an apocalyptic promise of eventual realization by the complete triumph of God, as Redeemer, over the sinfulness and imperfections of men, attended by the transformation of their, at present, imperfect environment. The idea of the Kingship of God became continuously enriched with the advance of prophetic revelation. His leadership over His people advanced in spiritual depth and intimacy. Its moral implications gradually threw off the limitations of inherited customs, of racial exclusiveness, of secular expediency. The divine Lordship over Israel was exhibited as springing from His Creatorship of the universe and His sovereign governance of its order as a marvellous yet growingly intelligible whole. The Kingship of God was not only supreme and living, but purposive. His purpose was universal in its scope and beneficent in its design. The special election of His people was intended to fit them to be His witnesses unto the ends of the earth. There should come a day, said one of the noblest predictions, when Israel should 'be the third with Egypt and with Assyria [her ancient foes], a blessing in the midst of the earth; for that the Lord of hosts hath blessed them, saying, Blessed be Egypt my people and Assyria the work of my hands, and Israel mine inheritance' (Isaiah xix. 24, 25). The Kingship of God is revealed as consisting not so much in the might and majesty of His Creatorship as in the adorable perfection of His character, and in His gracious relationship to His universe, especially to men who, made in His image, are capable of fellowship with Himself. His almighty power is the instrument of His Self-giving in grace and fatherliness, which make Saviourship the final manifestation of His glory.

Old Testament prophecy culminates on the very brink of interpreting the Kingship of God in terms of His Fatherhood. The bridge that joins the Kingship of God to the idea of His Kingdom is to be found in the fact that, according to the Old

Testament prophets, the character of God is revealed in the highest and holiest that man comes to apprehend, and seeks, at his best, to become. This highest and best is the indispensable foundation of the national and social order of life. The all-important task of statesmanship and patriotism is to secure the safety and well-being of the commonwealth by faithfully applying the values of divine perfection to the ordering of the common life, alike in its internal affairs and in its foreign relations. Yet, as has already been remarked, this does not exhaust the prophetic message. 'Holy is He.' God surpasses in His infinite perfection the highest vision that He can give to men. Man was made in the image of God; yet the image – because finite and frail – can only imperfectly, though truly, receive and manifest the glory of God. Only this inexhaustible Beyondness of the perfection of God can sustain His sovereign Lordship. Yet the holiness of God is revealed in His righteousness and merciful graciousness. Hence the commandment, 'Be ye holy, for I am holy', is not prohibitive and deterrent, but filled with the worshipful attractiveness of the attributes of God. Its meaning is finally displayed in our Lord's command, 'Ye shall, therefore, be perfect, even as your Father in heaven is perfect'. Holiness is the guardian of perfecting as self-fulfilment, and, therefore, as social.

III. THE KINGDOM OF GOD

The Idea of God and of His Kingship gives the key to the conception of His Kingdom. It is not to be treated as an external constitution, but as the establishment of the effective rule of God in the hearts of men, with all the beneficent effects which that rule can alone bring about. Everything depends, for the prophets, upon the knowledge of Jahweh and upon walking in His light. This is to say that the knowledge of Jahweh in the glory of His spiritual and ethical splendour, attained in living fellowship with Himself, sets up the standard for character and conduct. The divine illumination is given in order that men, in their personal conduct and their social relations, may apprehend, in all its fullness, the character of God, and may reproduce it throughout the life of the city and the State by reverent and ready response to Him, in the fellowship of complete oneness with Him, in heart, mind, and will.

In view of the sinfulness of men – their self-will, ignorance, and weakness – Jeremiah came to see that the fulfilment of this ideal required for its possibility an inner change in the spirit of the people. In the great prediction which anticipates the transforming gift of Pentecost, he says, 'This is the covenant that I will make with the house of Israel after those days, saith Jahweh: I will put My law in their inward parts and in their heart will I write it: and I will be their God, and they shall be My people: and they shall teach no more every man his neighbour, and every man his brother, saying, Know Jahweh, for they shall all know Me, from the least of them unto the greatest of them, saith Jahweh: for I will forgive their iniquity, and their sin will I remember no more' (Jeremiah xxxi. 33, 34). By this divine act of forgiveness and illumination the declaration of Deuteronomy will be verified –

'For this commandment which I command thee this day, it is not too hard for thee, neither is it far off. It is not in heaven that thou shouldest say, Who shall go up for us to heaven, and bring it unto us, and make us to hear it, that we may do it. Neither is it beyond the sea, that thou shouldest say, Who shall go over the sea for us, and bring it unto us, and make us hear it, that we may do it? But the word is very nigh unto thee, in thy mouth, and in thy heart, that thou mayest do it' (Deuteronomy xxx. 11–14).

Neither the world nor the city and nation, however, is static. The present situation, at its best, is a stage in the progressive development of the divine purpose. The social organism is in process of evolution through the living fellowship and partnership of God and man. Hence the prophet Joel predicts that 'It shall come to pass afterward that I will pour out My spirit upon all flesh; and your sons and your daughters shall prophesy, your old men shall dream dreams, your young men shall see visions: and also upon the servants and upon the handmaids in those days will I pour out My spirit' (Joel ii. 28, 29). Even this divine illumination and inspiration, however, will not be sufficient to bring about the ideal blessedness of the future. Transcendent divine action is necessary as well as the immanent influence of the Spirit of God. Hence Joel joins with the prophets in predicting 'the great and terrible day of Jahweh' (Joel ii. 31). The Kingship of Jahweh implies judgement upon evil, alike spiritual and material (for these are interfused), in order to open the way for the redemptive deed by which He will endow righteousness with blessedness, abolishing the mortality of men and transforming their cosmic environment. The Kingdom of God, therefore, involves at every point divine activity, the grace of His Spirit in the reconciliation, renewal, and illumination of men, together with the transcendent exercise of the power, by which new heavens and a new earth will be brought into being as the adequate and harmonious environment of perfected spiritual life.

What, then, are the practical demands of the Kingdom of God, realized in so far as rulers and people hearken to His voice? They are set forth in common by all the prophets, and are specially emphasized and applied by Isaiah and the later prophets, for whom the Kingdom found its centre in Jerusalem. Towards God, reverent faith and dedication, humility, teachableness, and obedience. They are for ever enshrined in the sublime utterance of Deuteronomy: 'Hear, O Israel: the Lord our God is one Lord: And thou shalt love the Lord thy God with all thine heart, and with all thy soul, and with all thy might. And these words, which I command thee this day, shall be in thine heart: And thou shalt teach them diligently unto thy children, and shalt talk of them when thou sittest in thine house, and when thou walkest by the way, and when thou liest down, and when thou risest up. And thou shalt bind them for a sign upon thine hand, and they shall be as frontlets between thine eyes. And thou shalt write them upon the posts of thy house, and on thy gates' (Deuteronomy vi. 4–9).

Towards man, the outstanding demands of the City and Kingdom of God are righteousness and mercy in all the relationships of life. In particular, the exercise of these qualities requires complete freedom from insolence and self-indulgence, from luxury and ostentation. Loyalty to authority, submissiveness to law, equity in commercial and industrial affairs, are essential. Equally obligatory is a merciful attitude in regard to helpfulness to the poor, the widows, and the fatherless. In general it may be said that the ideal of conduct in the Holy City is, 'Thou shalt love thy neighbour as thyself' (Leviticus xix. 18). To be the people of Jahweh meant the recognition that Israel is a family, bound together, not only by the tie of race, but above all by faith in Jahweh as so fatherly that His people form a community, in which fellow feeling, considerateness, and service should be as natural as they are binding. The outstanding characteristic of the Kingdom of God is that His service consists in the apprehension of His holy perfection and its manifestation in the ethical qualities and conduct which establish and sustain communal well-being. Micah speaks for all the prophets, as well as for himself, when he cries, 'Wherewith shall I come before Jahweh, and bow myself before the high God? Shall I come before Him with burnt offerings, with calves of a year old? Will Jahweh be pleased with thousands of rams, or with ten thousands of rivers of oil? Shall I give my first-born for my transgression, the fruit of my body for the sin of my soul? He hath showed thee, O man, what is good; and what doth Jahweh require of thee, but to do justly, and to love mercy, and to walk humbly with thy God?' (Micah vi. 6–8). The guardians of the Kingdom of God, of His City, are joyful worship, as uttered in the Psalms, reverent fear as the protection of loyalty and love and wisdom reflecting, not merely upon the prudential conduct of life, but on the highest values, as the divine foundation of a stable order of righteousness and truth, and finding in the pursuit of these values for embodiment in the human order, not repression, but liberty and life (Proverbs viii).

To sum up the teaching of the Old Testament. The Idea of God as spiritually and morally perfect supplies the authoritative ideals of personal and social life. For God is King, having a fatherly regard for, and relationship to, His creatures, and especially towards His people, which makes His rule not only authoritative, but the secret of peace and security, of love and life. His spiritual and ethical Kingship constitutes His Kingdom, which rests upon Him, manifests Him, and is sustained by His almighty power. His Kingdom is actually existent, and yet is still to come. Its coming depends upon the fulfilment of potentialities – spiritual, moral, and physical – which are already active in the world, because they are living in its Creator and Lord. The coming of the Kingdom of God, as the consummation of its present reality, will be brought about through the mediation of an ideally perfect King, in whom the perfection of God is completely displayed, and by the influence of the Spirit of God so transforming the hearts of men as to make them the reflection of His glory. This eventual Kingship of God is 'unto the ends of the earth', for His Universal Creatorship is manifested in the moral kinship, as Amos and Isaiah saw, which makes mankind prospectively one family in God. The spiritual renovation which will establish, after judgement, the inner Kingdom of God in the hearts of men, will be accompanied by the cosmic transformation, which will ensure to men, made God-like, complete redemption from evil, and participation in the eternal blessedness of God.

IV. OUR LORD'S REVELATION OF THE KINGDOM OF GOD

For the religion of the Old Testament, as has been seen, the Idea of God, in the holiness of His spiritual and ethical perfection, dominates the whole of human life. The spiritual and the social are organically and indissolubly bound up together. Sustained by worship, formulated by revelation, proclaimed by prophetic inspiration, social ideals consist in the application to all the concerns of life of the righteousness, truth, and mercy for which the name of Jahweh stands. The fulfilment of these ideals was, as time went on, seen to depend upon redemption, upon perfect atonement with God, and consequent renewal of the hearts of men by His Spirit. The perfecting of the spiritual and the social carried with it the necessity and the assurance of the final transformation of the universe, so as to make it the ideal home and instrument of the eternal perfection of God as conveyed to men through fellowship with Himself.

In what relation does this stand to the teaching and work of our Lord? In what sense did He complete it? And to what extent did He transform it? According to His own statement, His work was evolutionary, and not revolutionary. In so far as it was the latter, this was because the current piety and precepts of Pharisees and Sadducees both obscured and disfigured the essential meaning of the Law and the Prophets. 'Think not', our Lord said, 'that I came to destroy the Law or the Prophets: I came not to destroy, but to fulfil' (Matthew v. 17). The religious attitude of the 'scribes and Pharisees' was for our Lord in as acute opposition to the Law and the Prophets as to Himself. He proceeded, therefore, to give fresh and deepened emphasis to the inwardness and spontaneity of true religion, as springing from the intimacy of fellowship with God. His teaching pierced to the depths of the spirit and the heart of men, whence the springs, motives, and intentions of conduct arise. Character held the secret of conduct, and both character and conduct should be the natural and spontaneous expression of oneness with God as their source, and not of the sense of an apartness from Him, which needs to be bridged.

This transforming fulfilment arose out of our Lord's immediate consciousness of God as Father, and of Himself as the Son. This unique relationship, however, did not separate Him from mankind, but as 'the Son of man' He held such an equally unique relationship to all men that His divine office was to convey to men the Sonship which He enjoyed, with all the fullness of its spiritual, moral, and social significance. For our Lord, the Fatherhood of God was the supreme reality, which included His Kingship, and supplied to His sovereignty the motives and methods of perfect love.

Our Lord's revelation of the Kingdom of God is perfectly conveyed by the Lord's Prayer. The meaning of the Kingdom is revealed in its reflection from the faith and hope, the attitude and desires, of those who truly utter the prayer. The Lord's Prayer unfolds, in a living sequence, the meaning and consequences of the Fatherhood of God, as apprehended by His Son. The address to 'our Father, which art in heaven', sets forth at the outset His supreme and vital relationship to His supplicants. He is 'in heaven', and, therefore, transcendent. His exalted position conveys the sense of His holy perfection and of His illimitable resources. He is '*our* Father', and, therefore, there is a bond of family community between Him and His children which puts all the resources of His Personality, His Character, and His Lordship at their service, through His Grace, and for the purposes of His Love. Because He is 'our' Father, His children are a community in Him, and all self-seeking is excluded, not only from their petitions, but from their desires. He is so truly our '*Father*' that the approach to Him is inspired by unquestioning confidence, while the sense that He is 'in heaven' inspires awe and reverence and makes His glory, and not our wants, the object of our desires. Those who truly utter this prayer are already at home with God, and have been so uplifted above all selfishness and earthliness that they have attained to the standpoint of God, have no other concern than His glory, and look upon themselves as the loyal partners rather than the mere instruments of His purpose for themselves and for the world. They contemplate with trustful assurance the advancing fulfilment of His purpose, assured of its beneficence, and dedicated to be both the beholders and the servants of its fulfilment.

Hence, 'Hallowed be Thy Name' is the first petition, because everything depends, both for God and for men, in this fellowship of love, upon the holy attributes of His Name and upon the worshipful apprehension of them by His children. It is in full view of the Fatherhood of God and of His Name that the petition 'Thy Kingdom come' follows and is understood. The eventual triumph in human history of what is already being realized in spiritual experience is necessitated both by the Fatherhood of God and by the essential aspiration of His children. This consummation can only be reached when 'the will' of 'our Father' is actually 'done', by His activity energizing in and through His children, in fellowship with Himself. From all this it follows that 'as in heaven, so in earth' becomes the ideal upon which the faith and hope of the children of God are fixed, and to the realization of which, in all its many-sided demands and possibilities, their hearts and lives are devoted. Herein there can be no distinction between sacred and secular, between spiritual and social, for the will of God as 'our Father' is His 'will to all goodness'. Under the domination of this supreme object, all human needs sink to the desire of becoming and remaining fit for such doing of the Father's will for the coming of His Kingdom as will enable His children to be fellow workers with Him. Daily bread, forgiveness, and deliverance from evil are, in different ways, the indispensable conditions of the furtherance of the fatherly purpose of God by His children. And, in regard to all these, the self-seeking of individualism, whether for the meeting of spiritual or of material necessities, has been cast out by the brotherhood, which never intrudes the 'I', the 'me', the 'mine', but always presents 'our' common needs to the Father in the perfection of brotherly love.

The Beatitudes, which are indeed felicitations rather than benedictions, simply accord with the Lord's Prayer by the progressive delineation of the character which can find complete satisfaction in using it. One additional note is, however, added: 'Blessed are they that have been persecuted for righteousness' sake; for theirs is the Kingdom of Heaven' (Matthew v. 10). The Kingdom of 'our Father, which is in heaven' comes not by peaceful and unchallenged progress. As in the case of our Lord, so in that of His followers, 'the powers of darkness' withstand the army of light. Faith and loyalty can only be maintained and consummated by the willingness to endure and the actual endurance of sacrificial suffering for the truth.

What, then, are the new notes in our Lord's teaching regarding the Kingdom of God? They may be briefly expressed. The truth of the Fatherhood of God gives to the fatherliness of the Old Testament kingship a new importance. It is no longer a gracious quality, but the due expression of a supreme and constitutive relationship. Creatorship now stands for the self-giving of God, and the kinship, the affinity, of mankind to Him. The truths that are scattered throughout the Old Testament – as, for example, that the law of God is the life of man – are gathered together, concentrated in, and founded upon a vital spiritual relationship, which makes them not only congenial to it, but its natural constituents and concomitants. The parables of our Lord are, therefore, largely parables of growth, of fulfilment and transformation by growth, rather than of the external and mechanical organization which is imposed by will and maintained by power.

The transcendence of God as Sovereign is transformed by His immanence as Father. Grace is not merely shown from without, even though without be above, but is given and operates inwardly through the 'good seed' of the Kingdom and the transforming introduction of the leaven. 'The Kingdom of God is within you.' Its spiritual reinforcement and unfolding is the outstanding sign of the fatherly sovereignty of God, and the condition for the final exercise of His power in 'the restitution of all things'. All things are to be 'summed up' in Christ, and such a consummation must needs be primarily and comprehensively spiritual.

There are, however, two new features in our Lord's teaching of the Kingdom of God. In the first place, His personality reveals a mediatorship between the Kingdom and mankind that was only imperfectly anticipated even in the Old Testament prophecies of the Messianic King. Entrance into the Kingdom is through Christ. It is through the grace and atonement of the Son that men 'come unto the Father'. In the second place, the apocalyptic hope of the Old Testament becomes a subordinate and consequential feature of the New. The '*shall* come' of the former gives place to the '*has* come' of the latter, a change which sets the satisfaction of present experience in the forefront, and brings all the spiritual resources of the Kingdom within immediate reach.

It is beyond the scope of the present volume to elaborate these distinguishing features of the New Testament. They must, however, be carefully noted if our Lord's doctrine of the Kingdom of God is to be accurately apprehended. Our Lord's insistence upon rebirth from above as the condition of seeing the Kingdom of God is conclusive evidence, if this were needed, that He was no facile optimist. The parallel declaration in the Synoptic Gospels that entrance into the Kingdom can only be gained by those who become as little children, and this *by conversion* (Matthew xviii. 3), emphasizes the same truth. How could our Lord look upon men with easy optimism when the prevalence and gravity of sin ever weighed upon His spirit, and when He looked forward to the Cross alike as His destination and as His indispensable task, if the Kingdom of God was to be fully and finally established in the hearts of men and in their common life? Yet if the Kingdom of God can only come through crisis, it is also true that there is continuity in this consummation, and that the crisis is the means of bringing about and completing this continuity. The Sonship to God which rebirth brings about is the fulfilment of possibilities so immanent in human nature in virtue of its primal constitution that all that is great, and noble, and good in men is a presage of it. Redemption is fulfilment. St. Paul obviously teaches this truth when, in tracing the preparatory stages of human religion, he declares, 'Because ye *are* sons, God sent forth the Spirit of His Son into your hearts, crying Abba, Father' (Galatians iv. 6). Furthermore, all our Lord's teaching as to the Kingdom embodies both the Eternal and the Apocalyptic. The Kingdom is not set forth by Him as an earthly paradise, however spiritually and ethically conditioned. It is the Kingdom 'of heaven'. In coming to earth it does not lose its transcendence as alike the origin, the centre, and the goal of its earthly and imperfect manifestation.

'Eternal life' cannot be limited by a transient earthly existence. The blessedness of the Kingdom is not that of any terrestrial order. The service which seeks to assimilate earth to heaven, the society of men to the blessedness of God, is the forth-putting of spiritual activities which have God as their spring, and, therefore, eternity at their heart. The individual is not lost, but found in the community, and eternity is the true sphere of the individual. So an eternal order adequate to be the home of the sons of God is implicit as well as promised, since they are His heirs. The transformation of the Old Testament Sovereign by His Fatherhood has many vital consequences. But none is more vital than this – that life and immortality are brought to light by the gospel (2 Timothy i. 10), and that the Kingdom of the Father must needs transcend, though it includes, the earthly promise of its consummation.

Yet, though the existing material order of the universe is inadequate to be the abiding home of men made perfect, and awaits transformation, as St. Paul says, at 'the manifestation of the sons of God' (Romans viii), the witness of our Lord's nature-parables is significant. He treats the processes of nature and the activities of men in regard to them as being 'like to the Kingdom of God', showing that there is such affinity between the existing order and the heavenly order, that is and that is to be, that the earthly can be the outward and visible sign of the spiritual and heavenly. Thus there is a sacramental significance in nature. Its affinity with the spiritual and eternal makes it a means both of the approach of God to men and of exercising human personalities for their eternal inheritance in the Kingdom of God. This truth gives sanction to such efforts of men in using and transforming the natural order as may make it increasingly a fitting instrument and environment for spiritual and ethical life. And this without denying, or neglecting, the truth that our Lord's 'Kingdom is not of this world'.

V. THE CHURCH OF CHRIST AND THE KINGDOM OF GOD

When we pass from the Gospels, and still more when we pass from the Old Testament prophets to the Acts of the Apostles and to the Epistles of the New Testament, it is obvious that an extraordinary change has taken place. Nation and city have fallen into the background, and the relationship of the followers of Christ to them has become merely external, and, indeed, accidental. The cause of this change was twofold. In the first place, city and nation were hostile to the new faith, and persecuted it. They afforded, therefore, no sphere of personal responsibility or collective action to the new 'household of faith'. In the second place, an altogether new catholicity had become part of the Christian experience and outlook, so that the sphere of the Christian community altogether transcended the limitations of race, nation, and city. The effect of this change was to increase the strength of all the directly spiritual influences, which, by their very nature, welded the followers of Christ into a distinct community, united in an intimate fellowship unknown before. The Church of Christ came into existence, and the statement given in the Acts of the Apostles is that all the converts to the faith 'continued in the apostles' doctrine and fellowship' – the community of sharing (κοινωνία) – 'in the breaking of bread and the prayers' (Acts ii. 42). This statement is both confirmed and illustrated by the moral and social teaching contained in the precepts and exhortations alike of St. Paul, St. Peter, St. John, and St. James. Despite superficial differences of presentation, the ethics of the new community spring, for all these writers alike, out of a unique relationship to Christ Jesus and to God in Him, as creative of a new social relationship and giving effect to it by a new life, inspired and fashioned by love, as the meaning of love has now been revealed by our Lord. The complete catholicity of this new community was attained by stages and by a development, at times acutely controversial, by which the old Jewish limitations were in the end altogether superseded, so that St. Paul could say that in Christ Jesus 'there cannot be Greek and Jew, circumcision and uncircumcision, barbarian, Scythian, bondman, freeman: but Christ is all, and in all' (Colossians iii. 11). Elsewhere he even adds, 'There can be no male and female, for ye are all one man in Christ Jesus' (Galatians iii. 28).

This new catholicity was brought into being by St. Peter, by the evangelistic activities of the followers of Christ, as they became scattered by persecution, and, above all, by the missionary labours of St. Paul. The missionary success of the Apostle led, of necessity, to his teaching, and to its eventual summing up in the Epistle to the Ephesians. Under all these influences the Catholic Church came into existence, and occupied the foreground, apparently in place of the previous predominance of the conception of the Kingdom of God. Yet the Church, though a self-contained, was not an exclusive community, for its fellowship in doctrine, and its sharing in the Eucharist and in the worship, were offered to all men by the preaching. By the proclamation of the gospel, men of all peoples were invited, and even bidden, to enter into the new Commonwealth of Christ, which has now become, in actuality and earnest, the Kingdom of God. As such, the Church takes over all the privileges of the Old Testament community. It is 'a royal priesthood' (1 Peter ii. 9), a heavenly *civitas* (Philippians iii. 20), 'the household' of God (Ephesians ii. 19). Still more, it is a Body, 'the Body of Christ' (Ephesians i. 23). All these features of its inheritance are subordinated to, and incorporated in, a new family bond, with its fontal inspiration and governing ideal. The Fatherhood of God is reflected in the vital and all-comprehending relationship of Sonship, with its privileges, responsibilities, and social intimacy. 'If children, then heirs; heirs of God, and joint-heirs with Christ; if so be that we suffer with Him, that we may also be glorified together' (Romans viii. 17). Hence the duty of translating the Idea of God into the ideals of social life and service is not only carried over from the city and nation of the Old Testament prophets, but gains new depth, vitality, and world-wide range through the Fatherhood of God, enjoyed as a sure possession by His reconciled and heaven-born sons. It is from this standpoint that the question of the relationship of the Church of Christ to the Kingdom of God must be contemplated. The answer may be given in the terms used by the present writer elsewhere.[1]

'In what relationship, then, does the Church of Christ stand to His Kingdom? The answer most frequently made is that the Church is the appointed instrument by which the Kingdom is advanced, the means of its coming. This explanation contains an obvious and important element of truth, but it is insufficient, and, taken by itself, misleading. For a mere instrument is external to that which it manufactures. Its operation is, for the most part, mechanical, and it is laid aside when its task is completed. A Kingdom that stands for fulfilled Sonship cannot be brought about by such external, and, in the strict sense, accidental action; nor can such life as that which is realized or realizable in the Church be properly treated as a mere means of anything outside itself, however commanding and important. If the Church is to be the instrument of the Kingdom, the Kingdom being what it is, it must be something more.

'Others identify the Kingdom with the Church of Christ, and in support of their contention call attention to the fact that, whereas the Gospels are full of teaching about the Kingdom and make but scanty reference to the Church, it is the other way about with the Epistles of the New Testament. It is clear that apostolic teaching treats the Church as being the immediate sphere of Christ's Kingship. According to the Epistle to the Ephesians, the Church is the Body of Christ, and He is its Head. Its members are brought by adoption to enjoy all the blessings of

[1] *God, Christ, and the Church*, pp. 225–8 (Hodder & Stoughton), (from *Towards Reunion*, Macmillan & Co.).

divine Sonship, stand in vital relationship to the Son as their "living Head", and in Him are in such fellowship with one another that they are in process of coming "unto the unity of the faith and of the knowledge of the Son of God, unto a full grown man, unto the measure of the stature of the fullness of Christ". This is to say that the Church is a living organism, the development of which is by way of complete fellowship towards the perfect realization and enjoyment of the divine relationships in and for which it has its being. Hence the Church is, by its nature and constitution, equivalent to the Kingdom, and manifests it in so far as the Kingdom itself has, as yet, been spiritually realized. Yet, while this is true, it is not the whole truth. It must always be remembered that the Church, though a distinct organism and organization, is not self-contained and cut off from the rest of mankind. In the Epistle to the Ephesians, once more, St. Paul describes the objective of his Apostolate as being "to make all men see what is the dispensation of the mystery, which from all ages hath been hidden in God, who created all things". The content of this mystery is that "the Gentiles are fellow heirs and fellow members of the Body, and fellow partakers of the promise in Christ Jesus through the Gospel". The Church is indeed "a kind of firstfruits", and the very fact of its missionary calling and success shows that in it a gift of life and salvation is enjoyed of which all men are by their very nature capable. In other words, the Church is the earnest and anticipation of redeemed mankind, which is to be gathered together in Christ's Kingdom by being brought to the enjoyment of those divine relations of light, and life, and love, into which believers have already entered by virtue of their restored and fulfilled Sonship. Hence there is the prospect of a threefold fulfilment – of Christ's Kingdom, of His Church as coming to partake of His fullness, and thus made the means of ingathering and transforming mankind, and of mankind brought through the grace of Christ and the ministry of the Church, to the full enjoyment of the life in the Father, without which man's nature perishes and his achievements fail. And these three are one. None is without the others. The Church in which Christ's Kingdom lives and has its prophetic witness is, on this basis, an instrument of the Kingdom, but only in so far as it is more than an instrument – a living embodiment of the grace it conveys, by sharing its blessings with men who are divinely constituted to receive and enjoy them. Thus "the Kingdom of Heaven is like unto leaven, which a woman took and hid in three measures of meal until the whole was leavened".'

To sum up. The faith of Christ has inherited the spiritual faith and outlook of the Old Testament prophets. It has surrendered no part of this inheritance. The character of God still gives law and promise to the social ideals of His children. Yet the very fact of the Fatherhood of God and of its full enjoyment by the redeemed and Spirit-filled Church of Christ is the cause of a far-reaching transformation. The Kingdom is catholic. Its catholicity rests not only on the sovereign constitution of the Creator, 'Who made of one every nation of men' (Acts xvii. 26), but upon the Atonement made 'for the sins of the whole world' by Christ, and upon the activity of the Spirit of Christ, bringing men of all races and classes into one family and one citizenship in heaven. Hence the world-wide manifestation of the character of God has become, not merely mandatory, but the vital expression of the unity of mankind in the Son of God, and of a salvation that embraces both the individual and society, alike body, soul, and spirit, in prospect of the final consummation in which all will be perfected together.

CHAPTER III

HISTORICAL

In passing from the exposition of the fundamental truths and principles contained in the Old and New Testaments for the guidance of the Christian Church in its social ideals and endeavours, it will be well to start with a general statement before turning to the historical records.

The inner meaning of any spiritual movement is revealed above all in its characteristic life. It is to be estimated by its governing ideals, by what it does, and what it seeks to become. Its originating cause, its final expression, and the process by which it advances to this fulfilment, constitute the unity by which it is to be explained and valued. A great movement is interpreted, but not created, by its formal articles of belief and rules of conduct, for spiritual apprehension, urge, and influence lie deeper and are more comprehensive than the intellectual formularies by which its adherents are educated and held together. Its spiritual apprehension and consequent conception of the meaning of life and reality alone reach to the inmost springs of activity, inspiring, fashioning, and directing its endeavours. Hence the Christian faith – and, indeed, all religions – must be estimated and judged by their history, by the place they hold in the revelation of truth and the development of mankind.

At every stage of human development – whether

primitive or advanced – religion and the humanities have acted and reacted upon one another. But religion, just because it has arisen out of the depths of human nature, has been in the past the more active and constraining force, whether impelling or inhibiting, whether exerting a personal influence or providing a social bond.

Our modern civilization has been reared upon the slowly growing sense of the value of human personalities, of the worth of human society, and of these as vitally bound up together. Religious influences have played an immense part in bringing about this valuation and conjunction. In so far as they have done so, this result has only been possible because religious faith has become so deeply spiritual as to foster and fashion personality, so strictly moral as to reverence personal rights and interests, so rational as to provide collective guidance both immediately practical and reflective, in order that the meaning of the fundamental principles that should govern personal relations may be understood and their application to actual conditions may be growingly effective. It follows from all this that the Idea of God has of necessity been the key to all endeavours to bring a Christian civilization into being. A truly catholic theism of religion and thought has been essential to comprehensiveness of progressive activity. It may be justly claimed that, despite all the disappointing features of its history, the Christian faith has, by its very nature, been philanthropic. Its Founder 'went about doing good'. Its characteristic precept was 'to do good and to communicate forget not: for with such sacrifices God is well pleased'. Its greatest Apostle spoke of 'the philanthropy of God', and reminded his hearers that our Lord had said, 'It is more blessed to give than to receive'. Its final theological statement was, 'God is love'. Its typical description of the relationship of God to men was in terms of Fatherhood and sonship. That this relationship involved universal brotherhood was set forth by its closely knit unity of Eucharist, fellowship, and preaching, for the proclamation of the gospel was directed towards realizing such unity of mankind in Christ as to bring all men into the intimacy of fellowship of which the Eucharist was the outstanding sign and seal. The standing order of the Church was, 'Let us do good unto all men; and specially unto them that are of the household of faith', the prior claim of the latter being due, not to mere preference, but to intimacy of relationship, with its obligations and opportunities. The fundamental belief of the Christian faith is that mankind is potentially one community, that this community is to have its earnest in the life of the Church, and that its universal realization is to be brought about, not only on humanitarian grounds, but because, as St. Paul said, God is 'the Father, from whom every family in heaven and earth is named'; that is to say that the Fatherhood of God is the organic cause of consequent and corresponding family relationships of His creatures in Him.

Some further and more precise statement may, perhaps, be of advantage in regard to a subject that is of such vital importance. The following governing considerations should be borne in mind.

1. It is a fundamental belief of the Church of Christ that God has a supreme spiritual purpose in

His constitution and ordering of the world. This purpose, while it can only be completely fulfilled in the eternal 'Kingdom of Heaven', demands and has received an adequate manifestation and inauguration in human history, which both culminates in and springs forth from the advent of our Lord Jesus Christ. In Him the nature and promise of this Divine Purpose have been authoritatively revealed, and through His Spirit His followers are being progressively guided into 'all the truth'.

2. This supreme purpose of God is the full manifestation of His 'glory' in the self-giving of His love. His love, with all the inexhaustible riches of its meaning and resources, is the sufficient reason which unites the blessedness of His eternal perfection with the creative and redemptive process of His Kingdom, which brings together eternity and time, and transfigures the secular order by transcendent spiritual values. This divine self-impartation has for its end the bringing of creation into the full response of spiritual fellowship with Himself, described by St. Paul as 'the manifestation of the sons of God' (Romans viii. 19).

3. The 'firstfruits' and earnest of this final consummation are found in the experience of believers in Christ, who through Him receive 'the Spirit of adoption, whereby they cry, Abba, Father' (Romans viii. 15; Galatians iv. 6). This means that they are called to receive ceaselessly the gifts and graces of sonship in order to manifest and impart them. They become 'fellow workers with God' by witnessing to the glorious meaning of His Fatherhood as it has been revealed in our Lord Jesus Christ, 'the Son of His love'.

Hence the Church of Christ started on its historic mission equipped, fashioned, and inspired by the faith and ideals which have been examined in the previous chapter. This faith, with its ideals, are the truth, 'as truth is in Jesus' (Ephesians iv. 21).

1. The Church, at the outset, enjoyed a spiritual and social fellowship that was founded in the prophetic and apostolic faith which it received from Christ, its Lord and Head. It was a family and household. This intimate fellowship was still more closely and firmly cemented by a common task and a common conflict with external foes. The ignorance, superstitions, and divergent beliefs, the misunderstandings and contempt with which the Church was confronted, were made insidious as well as threatening, owing to the fact that its members came into 'newness of life' out of old habits and associations in which they had been brought up, and in existing relationships which tended to infect the new with the still persistent besetments of the old. The spiritual life that emerged was, therefore, affected, both in its triumphs and its shortcomings, by the inheritance of the past.

2. The Church was catholic from the first. It received converts of all races, classes, and religions into an equal brotherhood, which is described in its ideal by the apostolic writings, particularly St. Paul's Epistles to the Ephesians and to Philemon, and in its actuality by the Acts of the Apostles and the disciplinary portions of the Pauline Epistles.

3. The Church, in carrying out its commission, was both missionary and martyr. It was in charge of *the truth* – of God in Christ Jesus as loving,

redeeming, and seeking all mankind. Its governing impulse was to *share* the salvation it enjoyed with all mankind. This sharing meant the bringing of all its members and converts to participation in the spiritual, ethical, and social ideals which the Church had received from Christ. The standard of the interior life of the Church became for it the standard of life for all mankind, to be realized in all men through the gospel, and in preparation for the final consummation at the *Parousia* of Christ. That in pursuing its immense task of bringing mankind to acknowledge and conform to the universal Lordship of the crucified, risen, and ascended Christ, the Church was not led astray by any facile optimism is made abundantly clear from all the New Testament writings, and above all by the Apocalypse. The Church recognized that it had to wrestle, 'not only against flesh and blood, but against the principalities, against the powers, against the world-rulers of this darkness, against the spiritual hosts of wickedness in the heavenly places', as St. Paul so gravely and dramatically described the conflict (Ephesians vi. 32). Yet in this same Epistle the Apostle gave to the Church the enheartening declaration of the will of God 'to sum up all things in Christ, the things in the heavens, and the things upon the earth; in Him, I say, in whom also we were made a heritage' (Ephesians i. 11). It was, and is, indeed, a life-and-death struggle, but the issue is beyond doubt, and, therefore, the evangelistic mission, with all its spiritual and social meaning, is confirmed, and not weakened, by the arduousness of the age-long campaign.

In view of all this, it becomes evident that the

historic performance of the Church must be judged by the entire situation, and by vital, and not mechanical, analogies. Moreover, from the very beginning the task was complicated, not only by the factors that have been noticed, but by the necessity that the Church should organize itself as a permanent institution with its own distinctive corporate life. It was compelled to investigate the intellectual content of the faith in order to hold its own against conflicting and challenging philosophies. In carrying out this essential intellectual, yet spiritual, task the Church had to detect and absorb affinities whereever they were found, to criticize divergencies, and to display the superiority of the faith. Only in this way could the catholicity of the Church be made good. Thus an institutional, a theological, and a polemic stage of Church history was inevitable, and the nature of these concerns made them so prominent as to throw into the background of attention that, throughout this period, the Church was advancing by the superiority of life by which its members were secretly and unceasingly leavening the society of the cities and towns throughout the Empire, wherever they were found. It is by the Parable of the Leaven – its apparent insignificance, its activity, and, not least of all, its secrecy – that the spread and influence of the Christian Church, in the first ages, must be estimated.

In pursuance of this spiritual mission, the Church at once acknowledged, ignored, or defied, and yet sought to transform, the Roman Empire. At length the Empire, under Constantine, came to terms with it, with the inevitable mixture of profit and loss which recognition by the State involved. On the side of profit, Christian leaders sought to modify Roman law by more humane principles, created ministries of help and healing, amazed the pagan population by remaining at their posts in times of pestilence, when others fled, in order to help the stricken. St. Ambrose withstood the Roman Emperor Theodosius, and prevented him from entering the cathedral church of Milan until he had done public penance for his massacre of the Thessalonians. Later on, the monk Telemachus made an end of the inhuman games, in which the populace rejoiced, by casting himself to the wild beasts in the amphitheatre. These are only samples of the heroic efforts made by Christians to give effect to their Idea of God in social ideals.

Yet, on the other hand, the very victory of the Church led to its serious undoing. Henceforward the Church became divided. The multitude accepted Christianity as the formal successor to pagan religions, and thereby treated it, in the main, as a mere external *cultus*. The minority, who took the faith seriously, and especially its other-worldly and ascetic characteristics, withdrew from the world into the seclusion of monastic communities. The growing pessimism caused by ages of imperial decay, of barbaric irruptions, and exceptional calamities, invaded the Church, depressing the spiritual vitality of its ordinary members, and accentuating the sense of forlorn isolation in the religious orders. In spite, however, of these disasters, the faith of Christ ever and again reasserted its vital meaning in saintly and heroic lives, and not least of all in its social significance from time to time until the Reformation. The religious orders kept alive the torch of learning, taught, healed, and helped their neighbours, seeking to soften and transform the barbarous invaders of the Empire, and to remedy the disorders from their violence and from the chaos that ensued. The tragedy that marked even these priceless services lay in the fact that, owing to the prevailing decay of faith and disorder of life, the essential duties of all Christians became the almost exclusive concern of the religious orders, instead of the social service of the whole body of the Church. Monks and nuns, friars and sisters, retired to their conventual fortresses, from which they, or some of them, issued on their beneficent services. The common people were left to submit to priestly ministrations, and to practise, at the best, accepted virtues, without any sense whatever that they were called to the spiritual apprehension of the gospel and to a mission to advance the Kingdom of God among men. Yet, despite this disastrous and almost universal failure, the essential genius of the Christian faith manifested itself now and then, here and there. Wherever and whenever it did so, the glory of God, as revealed in Christ, was treated as the pattern, to be sought after by holiness, and to be set forth in devoted beneficence.

In general terms, the peoples and societies of Western Europe in medieval times may be described as the result of the fusion of indigenous races with barbarian invaders – Teutonic or Scandinavian – and with the permanent influence, varying in depth and range, of the Roman Empire and occupation. The great majority of the peoples dwelt in village communities, subject to overlords and to fixed customs of tenure, tillage, and labour. Their social order was for centuries unchanging. They were vexed – though not profoundly troubled – by ceaseless warfare and by compulsory contributions of personal military service, as well as labour, to their feudal overlords. The Church, which had at first been missionary, had long become the local representative of the papal autocracy, which claimed to hold the keys of the Kingdom of Heaven. The Holy Roman Emperor claimed to exercise a like authority in secular affairs also by divine right, as did the overlords, greater and lesser in descending scale, till the lord of the manor was reached. He exercised his rights, subject to the immemorial customs by which social and economic life was organized and controlled. This static and stagnant state of things was disturbed by the rise of the towns and the growth of commerce. The eventual advent of nationhood and of strong central government was hastened, and indeed was largely due to these changes, and to the problems, demands, and necessities that they brought about.

At the time when, as the result of long-continued decay and corruption, the influence of the Church throughout the West was at the lowest point, the Renaissance arose. The revival of learning, the recovery of Greek literature, the discovery of the New World, were accompanied by the rise of a new spirit of adventure, which, in giving birth to a process of adjustment to the new conditions, disintegrated what remained of the old order. The spirit of humanism awoke with a new sense of the values and possibilities of earthly life. Its secular world-view was set over against the deep gloom cast by the overshadowing and threatening conceptions of the other world, with the emphasis on 'the last things' – death, judgement, heaven, and particularly hell, which was the last weapon used by a decadent Church in a despairing attempt to subjugate men to ecclesiastical authority and to terrify them into decency of life. The secular view and the defiant adoption of Hedonism accompanied the determined attempt to revive the ideals of pagan Greece as the basis of naturalistic life, to the disregard, and even defiance, not only of the Church, but of all the spiritual and moral standards of the Christian faith. Yet, even in the case of this revolt, the power of the faith to discriminate between the good and the evil in the new movement was shown by such Christian humanists as Erasmus, Sir Thomas More, and Colet, not to mention other and less distinguished men. Such Catholic humanism was, however, utterly insufficient alike for the reform of the Church and the renewal of Christian life. For this regenerating work only the Protestant Reformation could suffice, with the consequent breach of unity in the Western Church. Only brief mention can here be made of the way in which, and the extent to which, the work of Luther and Calvin reasserted the authority and influence of the Idea of God in respect of the social ideals which dominated the Reformation.

It is obvious that Luther was set upon moral reform, as attendant upon, and bound up with, the evangelical experience of Justification by Faith. Yet he never freed himself from the dualism which he had inherited from St. Augustine, with its severance of the *Civitas Dei* from the secular order of the world. In a modified form this separation was upheld by Luther, who treated the State as having its own sphere of authority, over which the ruler was supreme. For him, the Pauline principle, 'the powers that be are ordained by God', remained unaffected by the new opportunities which the renewal of Christian faith and life afforded for the reformer, not only of the Church, but of the State. Moreover, he felt himself driven to seek the protection and to accept the authority of the ruler over against the tyranny and persecution of the Pope. Hence the disastrous adoption of the principle, 'Cujus regio ejus religio', with the subservience to the ruler and the subordination of the Church, which were its unhappy results. His repression of the peasants and his exclusion of politics from the sphere of the Church followed from this subservience, attended by alarm at the unforeseen and unpredictable consequences of the new social ferment to which his own teaching, as well as the conditions of the age, had given rise. It must also be recognized that Luther's exclusive insistence upon Justification by Faith only led him to trust too much to the 'liberty of the Christian man', to the neglect of the ethical instruction and guidance, which was consequentially insisted upon in the Epistles of St. Paul. His disparagement of the Epistle of St. James is striking evidence of this one-sided point of view.

With Calvin, as his government of Geneva shows, the case was altogether different. His religious individualism was combined with the claim of ecclesiastical supremacy over the State, with the object of imposing Christian ethics as cultivated in the Church upon the entire population by the autocratic power of the Church acting through the

State. It is clear that this tyrannical, and eventually abortive, attempt at ecclesiastical domination in ethical interests was due to Calvin's defective Idea of God, to the magnifying of His Sovereign Will, of which His elect were agents, to the disregard of His love and of the methods it employs. The promotion of popular education, by which the spread of Calvinism was attended, may in large measure be attributed, not to the acceptance of Christian humanism, but to the demands occasioned by the assertion of 'the right of private judgement'. If the authority of the Bible was to succeed that of Rome, it was evident that men must be enabled to study the Bible and that their 'private judgement' must be disciplined by such education as would enable them to understand it. This brief and somewhat cursory notice of the Reformation is all that can be attempted in this chapter. The main object of the author is to concentrate attention upon the Methodist Revival and upon subsequent religious movements, which have clearly demonstrated how the Idea of God has affected the social ideals of Christian people, and through them of England as a whole.

It has been a commonplace, not only of religious but of social historians, to attribute the rise of our modern philanthropy as being largely due to the influence of the Methodist and Evangelical Revival during the eighteenth and the early part of the nineteenth centuries. Throughout that period the callousness and hardness of preceding centuries, with their shocking consequences, were only slowly giving way to the rising temper of humanitarian sympathy and remedial beneficence. The social significance of Methodism arose from the fact that the spiritual transformation of John and Charles Wesley, with their fresh vision of the grace of God manifested in the Cross of Christ, tended steadily and surely to substitute the supremacy of divine and universal love for the austere conception of the Sovereignty of God, as magnifying His inscrutable Will, the external authority of His Law, and the irresistible ordination of His Providence over the conditions of terrestrial life. The emphasis upon 'Perfect Love' as the aim of Christian pursuit and the possibility of Christian experience was momentous, for, if its full significance be apprehended, it is clear that the very nature of Perfect Love makes its self-giving universal in its scope, comprehensive in its concern, and humane in its renovating influence.

This claim stands in need of somewhat full elucidation. Professor Whitehead has remarked that 'Methodism was singularly devoid of new ideas, and singularly rich in vivid feelings' (*Adventures of Ideas*, p. 11). This statement will probably be accepted, and even welcomed, by many Methodists, especially when the Bicentenary of the great experience that came to John Wesley in Aldersgate Street on May 24, 1738, has recently been commemorated, and, therefore, when renewed stress has been laid upon the fact that then his 'heart was strangely warmed'. Sometimes it is enthusiastically affirmed that Methodism is 'the religion of the warmed heart', and this emphasis has often led to its disparagement, and sometimes to its perversion, as chiefly concerned with emotions, and not with the objective truth of the Christian faith. Two criticisms of this mistaken impression must be made. In the first place, undoubtedly the evangelical experience of John Wesley was attended by the strange warming of his heart. Without this warming his mission could not have been undertaken at the outset, or carried on throughout the following half-century. Yet Wesley, with his keen intellectual activity, his pragmatic insistence on 'proving all things', and his combination of eager faith with searching criticism of its grounds, was the very last man to elevate mere 'feelings' to the supreme position that can only rightfully be given to reasonable faith. Moreover, only such reasonable faith fixed upon the gospel as divine and objective *truth* could have enabled him – a frail and sensitive man – to sustain the relentless stress, the ever-threatening dangers and difficulties, of his lifelong campaign. His frequent statement in his *Journal*, 'I offered Christ', as the description of his open-air preaching, shows that he was absorbed in proclaiming an objective *truth*, which transcended, yet was naturally attended by, emotional response from those who accepted it.

In the second place, Professor Whitehead's statement that Methodism was 'singularly devoid of new ideas' requires serious qualification. It is true that Wesley inherited the great tradition of New Testament, Catholic, and Reformed theology. He accepted its doctrines, emphasized their meaning, and, for the most part, moved within their boundaries. Yet the quality of *newness* extends beyond 'new ideas'. There may be a new emphasis, a new proportion, a recovery of what has been neglected and become obscure, which may effect as true and vital a revolution of thought as the importation of new ideas from without. Such newness was certainly characteristic of Wesley's teaching, both in the truths he asserted and in the consequences that he perceived. It was by means of this newness that the influence of Wesley has extended far beyond Methodism, notably in the abandonment of the rigours of Calvinism and in promoting a certain liberality in handling dogmatic doctrines. Only as a consequence of this newness of thought and concern, far more than of feeling, could Methodism have exerted the social influence to which attention will shortly be called. That the relationship of God to mankind has come to be conceived as that of universal Fatherhood is more directly due to the pervasive influence of Methodism than to any other spiritual cause. It has already been remarked that Wesley's explanation that Methodism simply proclaimed perfect love to God and to man, because this is the religion of Christ, revealed a secret of catholicity, humanity, and comprehensive concern that were new to the eighteenth century. His famous saying, 'The world is my parish', the measures that he took to meet the needs of his 'parish', and the philanthropic institutions that he founded, are evidence of this. There is also – what is equally important – the evidence that for John Wesley the distinction between the sacred and the secular hardly existed, if at all. The sacred, for him, sanctified and inspired the so-called secular. Thus, to an inquirer, he replied, 'Do all the good that you can, in all the ways that you can, to all the people that you can'. This spirit breathes in Charles Wesley's hymn:

Then let us attend
Our heavenly Friend,
In His members distressed,
By want, or affliction, or sickness oppressed:
The prisoner relieve,
The stranger receive,
Supply all their wants,
And spend and be spent in assisting His saints.

This was to preserve the old ministries of the Holy Club at Oxford, baptized into the new spirit of evangelical experience. An enthusiasm for doing good had been born. If at various points the broad and rich humanism of John Wesley was qualified by austerity, as, for example, in his educational efforts, this characteristic is to be explained not so much by his personal qualities as by the severity of his upbringing, by the laxity of his age, and perhaps, to some extent, because he was himself called to endure exceptional hardness, and, in doing so, to exercise severe discipline over himself. Of this necessity, the following entry in his *Journal* is witness. 'I found', he says, 'a natural desire, O for ease and a quiet resting place. Not yet, but eternity is at hand.' Throughout the whole of John Wesley's ceaseless spiritual and social activities the main stress was laid upon the Cross of Christ, as displaying the merciful and costly pity of God and His 'will that all men should be saved'. Hence the ignorant, the depraved, and the outcast were brought into the forefront of remedial efforts, which were not only spiritual and moral, but humane. It followed from this emphasis on divine *mercy* that the chief activities of evangelical philanthropy were directed to the remedy of obvious evils, and were palliative rather than reconstructive.

This drawback has been pointed out and severely criticized by recent historians, notably by Mr. and Mrs. J. L. Hammond. Yet certain qualifying considerations should be borne in mind. At the time of the Methodist Revival, and of the consequent Evangelical Revival in the Church of England, physical science and its practical applications were in their infancy; social science was non-existent. Democracy was unborn, and the organization of government, both national and local, was comparatively primitive. It was under these disabilities that the Industrial Revolution came about, unprecedented, unordered, individualist, and unmanageable. Individual enterprise reigned supreme, uninformed by knowledge and uncontrolled by the nascent, and as yet powerless, sense of community. The inherited love of liberty and intolerance of governmental interference affected all classes of society. Amid all these disabilities only palliative action was possible, only voluntary and spasmodic action was practicable. What the Revival supplied was a new and widely diffused motive and momentum, as an incentive, together with limited practical efforts as an example. These initiating influences prepared the way for the epoch-making work of the great Lord Shaftesbury, who, himself an evangelical, carried over the humane influences of the Revival with its voluntary efforts into the realm of parliamentary discussion and national legislation. This fuller, though imperfect, recognition of the responsibility of the State for the condition of the people was growingly promoted by the advent of democracy, the reform of Parliament, the rise of popular local government, backed by the advance both of physical and social science.

The charge is sometimes brought against Wesley that he was an 'individualist'. This criticism was, for example, repeated last year in a national broadcast address, in which the Rev. Joseph McCulloch paid an otherwise notable tribute to the great leader, in which he said that he could only be compared and classed with St. Paul and St. Francis of Assisi. To this charge it must be replied that Wesley was certainly not an individualist, if by that be meant that he was exclusively concerned with individuals as units. The salvation of *persons*, as individuals, and their perfecting in the Grace of our Lord Jesus Christ, was rightly the main object of his evangelism. But he said that he 'knew nothing of any solitary religion'. He also wrote, 'The gospel of Christ knows no religion but social, no holiness but social holiness'. When he discovered in certain religious societies a model from which the Methodist Class Meetings could be developed, he remarked, 'This is the thing, the very thing, we have wanted so long. Look east, west, north, and south, name what parish you please, is Christian fellowship there? Rather are not the parishioners a mere rope of sand. What Christian connexion is there between them? What intercourse in spiritual things? What watching over each other's souls?' This statement was lamentably true of the Church of England in his time. Hence, though careful to take part in the sacramental life of the Church and to enjoin the same observance on Methodists – from which, alas! they were commonly repelled – Wesley sought to create this essential fellowship between those who were of 'the household of faith' and knew themselves to be members of the Family of God. His Class Meetings became a Co-operative Society for sharing, on equal terms, the spiritual experience the members enjoyed, and, also, for ensuring that such help, including material assistance where necessary, should be available for every Methodist. Of such equality in later times the late Rev. W. H. Lax gave me the following delightful example. A mill-owner in the north of England was a member of a class that was led by one of his employees. On one occasion the leader came to see his master on Church business, and presented himself at the front door of the mansion. The servant ordered him to the back door, to which he always went when on the business of the mill. 'No, Mary,' was his reply, 'I am not on back-door business to-day!'

On reflection it will be seen that this emphasis on fellowship does not conflict with Professor Whitehead's definition that 'Religion is what a man does with his solitariness'. The supreme object of religion is communion with 'the Father of our spirits'. Yet when He is apprehended, in solitude, as 'the God and Father of our Lord Jesus Christ', the believer is sent forth from his 'solitariness' to share what he has received of the love of God in a service that, just because it is so deeply spiritual, must needs become frankly and fully social.

When we pass from John Wesley and the dawn of the Revival to the subsequent history of Methodism, a mixed, and in many respects disappointing and even disastrous, situation reveals itself. On the passing of Wesley, Methodism received into worthy but unequal hands a situation of unspeakable difficulty. On the one hand was the unexhausted mission committed to the founder, the prosecution of which was attended by continued success, especially in the industrial centres of the kingdom, but which also encountered unabated opposition from the Established Church – an opposition which was equally harmful to those who sought to remain within its borders, and to the multitudes who had been converted through Methodism having had little, if any, previous connexion with the Church. The necessary task of transforming a mission into an organized communion was arduous and lengthy. The institutional stage of Methodism inevitably set in, and had to be dealt with by the Conference of Wesley's Helpers, the itinerant 'Methodist preachers', or, as we should now say, the ministers. Thus the inherited Methodist administration had to deal with an immense lay movement, in which the spirit of democracy was awaking, owing in part to the stirrings of the national life and still more to the influence of Methodism itself, due to the responsibilities that it had cast upon lay leaders, local preachers, and other officers, not to mention the Methodist people as a whole. And this before the era of popular education! Is it any wonder that conflicts arose between authority and freedom, between 'preacher' and people, that scattered and disturbing movements arose, and that a series of secessions took place? Only gradually, and at great cost, could a Church polity be built up which would do justice to all the legitimate and inevitable interests of a body which had to become a Church while remaining a Society, had to prosecute a commanded and controlled mission while nourishing an equal fellowship of voluntary service.

Furthermore, the Industrial Revolution came into full being and proved seriously divisive in Methodism. The vigour, confidence, and self-discipline developed by Methodism enabled the abler men to take full advantage of the new commercial and industrial opportunities. Such successful men treated the highway by which they had advanced as equally open to all, and, therefore, frequently combined hard-faced enterprise with Church activities, and even with a measure of spiritual fellowship and benevolent philanthropy. They naturally became fearful of revolution, adherents of the current political economy, and supporters of those who, both in Methodism and in national life, were opponents of organic change. Their economic evolution withstood 'perfect love', the meaning and social implications of which became hidden from view. These features, which disfigured Methodism, are only part of the picture. The autocracy of the 'Old Body', of which Dr. Jabez Bunting was the practical dictator, cannot be defended, but needs to be viewed in the light of many qualifying considerations. The celebrated 'Liverpool Minutes' of 1820 show how profound was the solicitude of the Conference for the prosecution of the spiritual and evangelistic mission of Methodism, and how completely the life of Methodists was dominated by this concern. For the sake of this, every entanglement was to be laid aside – amusements and self-indulgence, of course, but also politics in revolutionary times. Justice must be done to this paramount object, to Methodist activity in promoting national education and other philanthropic undertakings; not least of all to the outstanding part which Bunting and Methodists took in the long campaign against slavery, throughout which their influence was increased owing to the very fact that their humanitarianism was free from any suspicion of party-political interests.

In regard to national education, the writer may be permitted to quote his grandfather, John Scott, the educational leader of Methodism in the early years of the Victorian era. Addressing the students of Westminster Training College in 1862 on 'The Working Classes entitled to a Good Education', he said: 'It has never been the manner of our community to call *Excelsior!* to the upper or "*lower* middle classes", content to leave the crowd grovelling below. Through the century or more of their existence, their great aim has been to promote the upward and onward progress of society, by directing an enlightened attention to the masses. Once they were nearly alone in this aim; they rejoice that now they are joined in it, and in active exertion to attain it, by a multitude of others, not of their own denomination.'

This, however, is by no means all that should be said. It is true that, though Bunting and the Wesleyan Methodist Conference were alarmed by the anti-religious influence of such men as Owen and Thomas Paine, with his *Age of Reason*, the forward movement of the industrial classes was to a large extent led by Methodists, and to a still greater extent permeated by Methodist influence. The industrial leaders, especially of the north of England, came largely from Methodist pulpits, classes, and Sunday Schools. Here they had learnt an Idea of God which shaped their social ideals and inspired their practical politics. They came forth from the school of Amos and Isaiah, rather than from that of the economic reformers. Thomas Hepburn, the leader of the miners of the Tyne and Wear, was a Methodist local preacher, as was also George Loveless, the leader of the 'Tolpuddle Martyrs'. These were the forerunners of a great succession, in which the names of Thomas Burt, Charles Fenwick, John Wilson, Joseph Arch, Henry Broadhurst, and Arthur Henderson stand out. Behind these men was a large body of obscure but influential men who, by the sheer force of their character and Methodist training, became the natural leaders of democratic movements, of economic and social progress. From these the early trade unionists and other reformers became acquainted with, and adopted, Methodist organization – its Classes, Societies, and even Camp Meetings – for their own societies.[1] Hence it has been very largely due to Methodism that, hitherto, the Labour Movement in England has been inspired by Christian faith and ideals, and has never become anti-religious.

Happily, this book is written when Methodist Union has carried into growingly progressive and harmonious effect a reconciliation and synthesis of manifold elements that were in conflict in Methodism throughout the nineteenth century. In the new fellowship and by the new instrument Methodism may, by the blessing of God, go forth to give such full effect through its faith and service, to the Idea of God as 'perfect love', as will maintain its transcendent 'citizenship in heaven' by pursuing fear-

[1] See the very important book, by Dr. Robert F. Wearmouth, entitled *Methodism and the Working-Class Movement* (Epworth Press, 8*s.* 6*d.*).

lessly and faithfully all those social ideals by which the life of heaven, of perfect love, may be progressively manifested upon earth.

It is beyond the scope of this volume to attempt to give even a sketch of the social ideals and activities that have sprung from the faith of Christ, even in England. Had this been possible, some account must have been given of the Moravians, the Society of Friends, and of the Dissenting Churches. The author's design has been restricted to an endeavour to trace the typical relation in which Christian theology has stood to social life during the first ages of the Christian Church, and then to call attention to such movements as have been of special importance in furnishing the social ideals and fostering the aspirations which have marked the rise of democracy in England.

Even this limited endeavour would, however, be lamentably incomplete without a concluding notice of Frederick Denison Maurice.[1] From the point of view of the relation of the Idea of God to Social Ideals, as in other respects, Maurice was the greatest English Christian leader of the Victorian era. 'A spiritual splendour,' Gladstone called him. He was prophet, philosopher, philanthropist, in a unique combination of religious genius. His philosophy, derived mainly from Greek and medieval sources, was too profound for the Church leaders of his day; his style too difficult, and sometimes obscure, for ordinary, even educated, men. Hence he was martyr as well as leader. Yet through his own

[1] For a fuller account the reader must refer to my book, *The Victorian Transformation of Theology*, being the Second Series of Maurice Lectures delivered at King's College, London, during the Lent Term, 1934 (Epworth Press, 2*s*. 6*d*.).

travail of spirit, with the help of Charles Kingsley as popular teacher, and assisted by a select band of practical intellectuals, he was enabled to effect a salutary and essential transformation of theology, and to give practical expression to the social principles and sympathies that were inspired by his spiritual vision in the foundation of his Colleges for Working Men and Working Women, in launching the Co-operative Movement, by which he hoped that competition might be superseded. In addition he stimulated all the best minds, in Church and State, that were directed to the uplifting of the whole people, through the establishment of a truly Christian commonwealth of spiritual, intellectual, and social sharing.

Brought up as a Unitarian, coming into contact with Calvinism, and faced by Tractarianism, Maurice reacted against them all, and eventually found his abiding spiritual home in the great passage of St. Paul: 'Giving thanks unto the Father, who made us meet to be partakers of the inheritance of the saints in light; who delivered us out of the power of darkness, and translated us into the kingdom of the Son of His love; in whom we have our redemption, the forgiveness of our sins: who is the image of the invisible God, the firstborn of all creation; for in Him were all things created, in the heavens and upon the earth, things visible and things invisible, whether thrones or dominions or principalities or powers; all things have been created through Him, and unto Him; and He is before all things, and in Him all things consist. And He is the head of the body, the Church: who is the beginning, the firstborn from the dead; that in all things He might have the pre-eminence. For it was the good pleasure of the Father that in Him should all the fullness dwell, and through Him to reconcile all things unto Himself, having made peace through the blood of His Cross; through Him, I say, whether things upon the earth, or things in the heavens' (Colossians i. 12–20).

Upon this great statement, together with the Johannine writings, the entire life, thought, and work of Maurice were reared. Hence, for Maurice, the eternal and universal Fatherhood of God, the eternal and divine Sonship of Christ, with whom the Father is One, the creative constitution of the universe in and for the Son, His Incarnation in the fullness of the times, and the redemption wrought for all men by His Cross were the constellation of the truth that was 'the light of all his seeing'. The eternal and incarnate Son of God is the root and ground of the community of mankind which has been spiritually constituted in and unto Him. Universal brotherhood was based upon the divine Sonship of mankind, as constitutive of a universal Commonwealth, to be progressively realized throughout the entire realm of human life. Hence the essential values of all individuals in the fellowship of society – as thus constituted by and for the Father, in and unto His Son – were to be realized by reconstructive and truly redemptive effort, embracing all the concerns of human nature in due proportion, and substituting co-operation for competition, sharing for dividing, in every sphere of life. And all this because 'the pattern' of the earthly Commonwealth is 'laid up in heaven'. It follows that God – the Holy Trinity – Truth, and Wholeness may be treated as the three conjoined watchwords which guided Maurice throughout his thought and work. Grace, and not sin, was the first word of human history, and would be the last. The Truth was the heritage of all men, as it was the crying need of all. Wholeness was the fruit of the Truth, and, therefore, truth must be sought and welcomed wherever it could be found, and brought to its consummation and synthesis in the catholicity of Christ. Redemption works with and through fulfilment. The aspirations of men can only be satisfied in the Kingdom and City of God, since they have their source as well as their end in the Father and in His Eternal Son. The Incarnate Lord is the Head of a new – and yet old – community, destined to embrace mankind and to be eternal in the heavens. It was in the radiance of this vision that the best men and women went forward to become the spiritual and the social leaders of the following generation. The Idea of God had in wondrous measure bestowed the social ideals for a new age of faith.

CHAPTER IV

RECENT

THE RESTRICTION of this historical survey to this country, in so far as modern social developments are concerned, is all the more necessary in giving some account of the social progress of recent times. That the Christian Church has been challenged throughout the past century by many social reformers is too obvious a fact to need either statement or illustration. Many of those who have been possessed by the 'enthusiasm of humanity' have not only claimed independence of it, but have proclaimed their hostility to it. The immense progress of the natural sciences and the advent of democracy have enabled and encouraged them to promote their social ideals upon the basis of a naturalist or humanist philosophy. Yet to a large extent the weapons with which the Church has been attacked have been supplied by the Church itself. The fundamental principles of the Christian religion have been used to exhibit the shortcomings and departures from them of which professed Christians have been guilty. And, what is of equal importance, secularist reformers have inherited the Christian tradition. They have indeed sought to found their endeavours upon a naturalist view of the universe. Yet the presuppositions upon which they have proceeded will be found, on examination, to depend upon assumptions for which materialist science and necessarian philosophy afford no justification whatever. The assumptions in regard to evolution, which were easily adopted throughout a period of material prosperity and progress, have been rudely shaken by recent history. The confidence in the immanent rationality and purposiveness of the universe, in the essential good nature of mankind, which animated the Victorian age, can only be supported by faith and by a hopefulness which draws its inspiration from sources for which materialism can give little or no justification, and which the course of events has dramatically contradicted. Instead of confidence in the sufficiency of civilization, men are, at present, haunted by the fear that the very existence of our present civilization is in danger, and that its destruction will come by the hands of the men who have inherited it. Hence the Victorian and subsequent eras have lived upon the religious inheritance of the past, and have been occupied, often unconsciously and in spite of themselves, in developing and applying the principles, the assumptions, and the sympathies with which it has furnished them. This conclusion must needs be the preface to our review of the facts and influences by which it was brought about.

The following events laid the foundation of the social progress, the determining factors of which we have now to consider.

1. In the first place came the carrying over of the growing humanitarian concern of philanthropists to the sphere of politics and social administration. Of this all-important and beneficent revolution, Lord Shaftesbury was the great leader. The great struggle which brought the Factory Acts into being is

sufficient evidence of the momentous change in public opinion and politics that was thus brought about. To effect it, Lord Shaftesbury was compelled to sacrifice his prospects of a great political career, and his motives were obviously evangelical. An outstanding leader in evangelistic and philanthropic enterprises, he carried these interests and concerns into the field of legislation. Side by side with this great achievement must be set the strenuous efforts of Christian educationists to convince Governments and Parliament that the education of the people was a national, and not merely a private, responsibility. This recognition was, at first, tardy, parsimonious, and restrictive, and only through religious leadership did it become effective. Thus the spirit of evangelical humanity became extended to the control of industrial undertakings in order to secure the protection of the weak, and the improvement of the health of the manual workers. The sphere of governmental and parliamentary responsibility was extended beyond that of national order and safety, to the positive obligation of securing the conditions of human well-being. The hitherto unquestioned autonomy of economics, industry, and commerce was destroyed. And all this at the dictates of evangelical faith, when as yet there was no democracy to bring about this dethronement.

2. Next in order came the Education Act of 1870, with its recognition, brought about by religious pioneers, that every child has a right to receive education, though its range was for a time more narrowly restricted than the more generous provision which Christian educationists had already brought about here and there by their voluntary

exertions. Compulsory school attendance and free education came about, in due course, as the sequel to Mr. W. E. Forster's legislation.

3. The extension of the franchise in 1884, prepared for by popular education, brought democracy into being, save for the enfranchisement of women, which was not conceded until their exertions and sacrifices in the Great War had at last convinced a reluctant Parliament of their true and essential citizenship. The reform of local government followed in 1888, and County Councils and District Councils thereby came into being on a completely democratic basis.

All these changes combined to make the British people responsible for their social well-being, in so far as this can be brought about by law and public administration. As the result of them, women came to play a steadily increasing and beneficent part in public administration. Their great leaders thereby evinced the qualities and gained the influence which, in the end, secured the enfranchisement of their sex. Thus, by successive stages, the machine of national and social well-being was, in its main features, perfected.

Yet a machine, however perfect, is useless unless it be set in motion and directed. The human machine, in particular, can only be set in motion and directed by ideals and influences which, even if impelled by necessities, are yet fundamentally spiritual. The sources and nature of these ideals and influences can be briefly stated.

1. The unexampled progress of the natural sciences and of the arts by which scientific knowledge was applied to human life need only be noted, as having

contributed the indispensable means of social progress.

2. As the result of this advance, and of the doctrine of evolution which accompanied it, what may be called the dynamic view of the world replaced the static, and was applied to the whole range of human concerns. In particular, the sense was brought about that the environment of mankind – the term being used with the widest implications – has not been fixed from creation, but that it may be progressively and immeasurably modified for the well-being of the human race.

3. A new sense of the urgency of 'the Condition of the People' question came into being, and of this as imposing a special responsibility upon the privileged members of the community, whether privileged by wealth, or by education, or by leisure. This new sense was created and fostered, not by the multitude, but by prophetic leaders in Church and State. The rise of the Salvation Army, the publication of *The Bitter Cry of Outcast London*, the movement of what may be called missionary education in the universities, even the Charity Organization Society (conceived as not merely disciplinary for thoughtless givers and importunate beggars, but as re-creative in its aim), may be instanced as among the influences which brought about and extended this sense of urgency and responsibility. The administrative experience of School Boards gave rise to the conviction that the ends of education cannot be attained in the schools, apart from securing the nutrition, the health, the housing, and the amenities which are essential to the well-being of the child population.

Under all these influences, the London County

Council came into being. Those who inaugurated its great career and laid the permanent foundations of its administration were not mere politicians. They had a truly – and for the most part a specifically – Christian concern for the well-being of London, and especially for remedying the mean, sordid, and distressed condition of its poorer districts by arousing the sense of community in the well-to-do. It is no exaggeration to say that the policy and programme of the council, in its formative period, were supplied by religious leaders and sustained by religious influences.

4. To what were these influences due? It may safely be replied, to the ascendancy of the religious Idea of the Fatherhood of God, taken in its simplicity, as derived from Christian faith. The sense of its universality, of the divine concern for men, in the wholeness of their nature, of the Fatherhood of God as the vital ground of the consequent brotherhood of men, with all the social obligations of brotherhood, inspired the reforming ideals and efforts of those who led the advance of social progress throughout the closing years of the nineteenth century. In London, Cardinal Manning, Hugh Price Hughes, Benjamin Waugh, W. T. Stead, and Samuel A. Barnett were the outstanding leaders of social advance. In the universities, the philosophy of Thomas Hill Green inspired such men as Henry Scott Holland, Charles Gore, and Edward S. Talbot in Oxford. In Cambridge, Professor James Stuart became the pioneer of the University Extension Movement. John Brown Paton, Congregationalist and social enthusiast, was a ubiquitous influence. Josephine Butler, Millicent Fawcett, and other

noble women were in the forefront of the movement. All these had a great following in the Church, in Parliament, in local authorities, and in philanthropic enterprises. Most of them had been directly, and all of them indirectly, influenced by Frederick Denison Maurice and by the Christian Socialism he brought into being. All, therefore, derived their Social Ideals from their Idea of God. Through them, above all, the great social advance of the closing years of last century was brought about.

There is, of course, another side of which due account must be taken. During the latter part of the nineteenth century the representatives of natural science assumed and proclaimed its all-sufficiency. They claimed that the then dominant abstractions, matter and motion, contained the complete secret by which the universe could be explained. This confidence has by this time given place to more moderate claims and to a greater humility. This change has been brought about by philosophical criticism, by the ever-changing concepts by which the natural sciences are directed, and, not least of all, by the growing sense of human, and indeed spiritual, values, which are not amenable to merely physical explanations. The very fact that T. H. Huxley coined the term 'Agnosticism' in order to shut off from scientific, and even philosophic, knowledge all that man is most concerned to know, is evidence of the impasse to which the physical sciences were brought when they claimed to furnish a complete explanation of the universe.

The result, however, of the exorbitant claims made on behalf of natural science and of its triumphs in the material sphere was naturally to strengthen the secularist spirit which became prevalent with practical and unreflective men, and is still widespread.

Moreover, an important change took place in the political world just when its social aims were becoming predominant. The Labour Movement took its rise in the north of England, where the influence of Methodism was most powerful. The great leaders, Thomas Burt, Charles Fenwick, John Wilson, and, at a later time, Arthur Henderson, were all cradled in Methodism, as were Joseph Arch, the leader of the agricultural labourers, and Henry Broadhurst, the first 'working man' to enter a British Government. As time has gone on, however, the centre of the Labour Movement has moved south, and the influence of materialist economics has tended to displace that of the prophets of the Old Testament and the guidance of the New. Yet both the scientific thinkers and the political leaders were steeped in the evangelical tradition. The presuppositions and the confidence of both were inherited from the past. They were more indebted to the Christian faith than they recognized. This was, above all, true of the multitudes to which the politicians appealed. As Mr. Charles Booth noted in his great work on *London Life and Labour*, the influence of the Evangelical Revival was still evident in the outlook, however vague, of the industrial classes of London. Hence the striking fact that purely secular education has never found favour, despite the religious controversies that have so unhappily taken place. Until recently, the cry that 'he wants to take the Bible out of the schools' was sufficient to bring about the defeat of any political candidate, even in London. This attitude has been so persistent and widespread that the issue has, by this time, ceased to be raised either in London or elsewhere. Every local education authority throughout the country is now concerned to provide and to improve instruction in the Bible. Hence religious leadership has continued to be potent in social politics, and the Idea of God, even if faint and indeterminate, has continued to move the British democracy with the confident hope, the sympathies, and the demands, which lead to ordered progress towards better things.

Special mention must be made of the Settlement Movement and of its great originator, Samuel A. Barnett, the founder of Toynbee Hall in Whitechapel, the first of the University Settlements. This movement could only have come into being under the spiritual and social conditions which have been described. It came about as the result of a remarkable combination between Balliol College, Oxford, under Jowett, and St. Jude's, Whitechapel, under Barnett. This combination was brought about mainly by Arnold Toynbee.

Toynbee was a brilliant young economist, whose teachings and writings did much to rescue political economy from the reproach of being 'the dismal science'. He was the author of the term 'The Industrial Revolution', which has come into general use. His intellectual interests and his humane sympathies led him to seek intimate acquaintance with the life of the poor in London, and, following the example of Edward Denison, a young M.P. who took up residence in the East End in 1867, Toynbee came to divide his time between Oxford and Whitechapel, thus coming into close friendship with Mr. and Mrs. Barnett at St. Jude's. Through Toynbee the Barnetts were introduced to the Balliol 'set', and close intercommunication was thus set up between the college and St. Jude's. Barnett, who, among his many social activities, had already taken a leading part in organizing University Extension work in the East End, and had Maurice's *Working Men's College* well before his mind, took advantage of Toynbee's early and lamented death to perpetuate his memory by a permanent institution designed to bring about a partnership between the universities and the East End, based upon, and embodying, 'the method of friendship', as distinguished from existing missions to the poor. In pursuance of this design he read a paper 'On Settlements of University Men in Great Towns' at St. John's College, Oxford, on November 17, 1883. The ground was prepared, not only by the example and influence of Toynbee, but by the impression created by such appeals as that of *The Bitter Cry of Outcast London*, the articles on 'How the Poor Live' which G. R. Sims contributed to the *Daily News*, and the forceful advocacy of W. T. Stead in the *Pall Mall Gazette*. As the result, Toynbee Hall was established in 1884 and became the forerunner of the many Settlements which sprang into being in London and other great cities of the United Kingdom, and also, through the great leadership of Jane Addams at Chicago, in the United States.

The genius of the Settlement Movement is best illustrated by studying the character and outlook of its founder. Samuel A. Barnett was so remarkable a personality that Clemenceau spoke of him as one of 'the three great men' he had met in England. He was not a dogmatist in his religious beliefs, and still less was he an ecclesiastic in his interests and connexions. For him, the Fatherhood of God was the substance of his faith and the foundation of all his endeavours. He held constant communion with Christ, as the revealer of the Divine Fatherhood and the Ideal Man. When asked by his wife, 'Do you believe in a personal immortality?' he replied, 'I can imagine life on no other basis'. Hence he confronted the squalid poverty and ignorance of Whitechapel with a vivid and steadfast sense of the kinship of men with God, and with the spirit of sharing the best values of life, which can only come from perfect love.

Barnett was supremely concerned, not with abstract theories or mechanical administration, but with human personalities, their development, and their safeguarding by a transformed environment, both material and social. He believed in, and sought to draw out, the best in all men, and especially among the poor of the East End. They were to be respected, not patronized or pauperized. They were to work out their own salvation, and this effect was to be stimulated by bringing the highest values of Truth, Beauty, and Goodness within their reach and to their apprehension. The universities were the historic storehouses of these values. They held them in trust for mankind. They should be shared by the overflow of their best minds in friendship and neighbourhood with the poor. In this sharing they would not be impoverished, but enriched.

Barnett was profoundly indebted throughout to

the brilliant comradeship of his wife, whose superb qualities of confidence, energy, and social gifts were indispensable for the overcoming of the humility, diffidence, and shyness of her husband. As the result of this partnership, Mr. and Mrs. Barnett published a joint volume of addresses and essays, entitled *Practicable Socialism.* In this book, emphasis was laid upon the sharing of the highest spiritual values and upon such reforms as would bring the treasures and instruments of these values effectively within the reach of all as the true and practicable end of human society, and in contrast to materialist and merely external Socialism. Such was the inspiration that originated the Settlement Movement, and, though Toynbee Hall was founded on a secular basis, in order that all men of goodwill might take part in this sharing, it is abundantly clear that the Idea of the Fatherhood of God was the source of the social ideals for which it stood.

Oxford House in Bethnal Green, the Women's University Settlement in Blackfriars, Mansfield House in Canning Town, Hull House, Chicago, and the Bermondsey Settlement sprang into existence soon after Toynbee Hall had led the way. The story of the Bermondsey Settlement has been told elsewhere,[1] and need not be repeated here.

Fifty years ago, on December 26, 1887, the proposal to establish the Settlement was laid before Dr. W. F. Moulton, at the Leys School, Cambridge, and received his instant approval and constant support. Bermondsey was eventually chosen as the neighbourhood in which it should be placed, as being, at that time, the least helped of the poorer

[1] In the author's book, *My Guided Life* (Methuen & Co.).

districts of London. Owing to circumstances, there was some inevitable delay in carrying out the scheme, but in 1889 it received the warm support of Methodists in the Universities of Cambridge and Oxford, and, with the approval of the Wesleyan Methodist Conference, a site was secured, the central building erected, and the work started at the end of 1891.

The following general aims were laid down at the outset by the warden:

1. To bring additional force and attractiveness to Christian work.
2. To become a centre of social life, where all classes may meet together on equal terms for healthful intercourse and recreation.
3. To give facilities for the study of literature, history, science, and arts.
4. To bring men together to discuss general and special social evils and to seek their remedy.
5. To take such part in local administration and philanthropy as may be possible.
6. And so to do all this that it shall be perfectly clear that no mere sectarian advantage is sought, but that it shall be possible for all good men to associate themselves with our work.

To these general aims the Bermondsey Settlement has adhered throughout its history, and in this spirit its manifold agencies have been carried on. The work has passed through successive phases, as the needs of the neighbourhood have varied. It has included evangelism, theological and biblical teaching, education, social welfare, and local administration in its programme. From the first the work of women has been indispensable to its success. It has had to surmount great difficulties, and, as is the case with all human institutions, it has fallen short of its high ideals. Yet the Bermondsey Settlement remains in full vigour, and is still, in many ways, indispensable to the welfare of the neighbourhood, and especially of the waterside in which its centres are placed.

The present tendency, active in the extreme sections of the Labour Party, is to react against the conception upon which the Settlements have been based. The class self-sufficiency of the industrial majority is a tenet that, perhaps naturally, is widely held. To destroy the present system, in order to a more satisfactory reconstruction, is the avowed aim of a minority by whom 'class consciousness' is fostered. The policy that is thus originated and stimulated contradicts the fundamental principles of social wholeness, of ordered process, and of mutual self-giving, upon which the Settlements have rested, and which they have sought to embody in their work. The result of this contradiction is to engender practical materialism, with its trust in mechanism, its externality, and its reliance upon the force of mass movements directed to political action. It remains true, however, that true progress must be spiritual in order to be truly social, and that it must be God-centred in order to call forth the best in men in fellowship with one another because they are in fellowship with God, and in partnership with His ordered purpose for mankind. Hence, if disaster and disappointment are to be avoided, social ideals must still be dependent upon, and inspired by, the Idea of God, as this has been given in our Lord and Saviour Jesus Christ.

CONCLUSION

THE COURSE marked out for this volume has been covered, and only a few concluding words are needed.

Humanism is as inadequate as materialism to supply the standards, the motives, and the ideals which are essential to the social progress of mankind. Humanity cannot stand self-enclosed in a universe which is alien from, and eventually hostile to, the highest ideals of men. Man is dependent upon the Reality from which he springs. The eternal, and not the temporal, must be in his heart, if the possibilities of the temporal order are to be achieved. A transcendent source must supply the standards and the example from which human ideals are derived and by which they are fostered and directed. The desires and movements of men must be *judged* from above, as they emerge from within. The sense of 'oughtness' must inspire and control the endeavours of men. This sense must be recognized as the Categorical Imperative of God, not as the mere mass-mind of men. Only God in Jesus Christ can meet the need, because in Him alone is the eternal and basal truth. Through and unto Him alone can human progress become at once catholic and personal, spiritual and social, evangelical and ethical, righteous and merciful, pure yet compassionate and redemptive. If mankind is to be saved and human nature to be fulfilled, the Eternal Love of God must be 'shed abroad' in the hearts of men below, that, through perfect love, the eternal values may be so fully disclosed and so truly shared that human life may become Life indeed.

9 781532 635090

www.ingramcontent.com/pod-product-compliance
Lightning Source LLC
La Vergne TN
LVHW010932100826
845153LV00001B/3

* 9 7 8 1 5 3 2 6 3 5 1 0 6 *